Matt Skinner

Heard it Through the Grapevine

Matt
Skinner

Heard it
Through the
Grapevine

For Carls and Indi
xx

Heard it Through the Grapevine
Matt Skinner

First published in Great Britain in 2008
by Mitchell Beazley
An imprint of Octopus Publishing Group Ltd,
2–4 Heron Quays, London E14 4JP

Distributed in the United States and Canada by
Octopus Books USA:
c/o Hachette Book Group USA
237 Park Avenue, New York, NY 10017 USA

An Hachette Livre UK Company
www.hachettelivre.co.uk

ISBN   978 1 84533 4833

Commissioning Editor Becca Spry
Art Director Tim Foster
Deputy Art Director Yasia Williams-Leedham
Design Concept The Plant
Designer Colin Goody
Photographer Chris Terry
Project Editor Georgina Atsiaris
Copy Editors Hilary Lumsden and Sam Stokes
Production Lucy Carter
Proofreader Siobhan O'Connor
Indexer Diana LeCore
Americanizer Caitlin Doyle

Set in Typ 1451
Printed and bound by Toppan Printing
Company, China

Contents

8 Introduction

12 Shopping

Starting points/Where to shop for wine/The bottle/The wine

56 Drinking

Love what you drink/Serving wine/Tasting wine

92 Eating

Trial and error/The rules/How to match food and wine/Matches to try at home

130 Sleeping

Fatal attraction/The opened bottle/The unopened bottle/
The cellar/The investment

166 Well-being

174 Glossary
175 Index

In the beginning, all wine was created equal

It was just a drink. Grapes were grown, harvested, crushed, fermented, bottled, and drunk. End of story. There was no wine culture to tangle yourself up in, no pretty labels to be baffled by, no fancy wine speak to learn, and no tricks to make choosing any easier. There was no choice. There was just wine. You drank it.

Then something happened. Wine became a salable commodity—a popular one, too—a product with real value. It became clear that particular countries were better at producing wine than others—but it didn't stop there. Particular areas within particular countries were better than others. Particular producers within particular areas were better than others. Particular wines from particular producers were better than others.

It became clear that there were lots of "particulars" and just as many "others," and that's when wine stopped being simply a drink and became something far more complex.

The more I learn about wine, the more I realize how much I don't know, although along the way I have encountered endless pieces of good advice, great tips, and genuine pearls of wisdom that have helped fill some gaps—the kind of practical information that anyone can use to help them get more from wine. That's what this book is about.

Without spending a fortune, or years of study, there are dozens of ways you can improve your wine experience. This book is about making more of an effort: what you put into wine is largely what you can expect back. And, should you decide to read on, I hope you'll realize that wine is an amazing drink made better by even just the tiniest of efforts.

Happy drinking!

Shopping

Starting points

Have you ever found yourself standing in the wine store, staring at the vast expanse of bottles in front of you, yet not really looking at anything at all? You desperately want to try something new, and want nothing more than to leave with anything other than that same old safe option you always end up buying. As you stare, you picture a different you, a wine-savvy you, strutting confidently and knowledgeably along the wine section. The wine-savvy you bypasses the special offers, heads for an exotic-sounding country, picks up an exotic-looking bottle of wine made from an equally exotic-sounding grape variety, scans the label, checks the price, smiles, and leaves—easy as that. As the real you reaches for that safe option—the one you bought a week ago and will probably buy again next week— that real you can't help wishing you were a bit more like the wine-savvy you.

You might not be as far from that wine-savvy person as you think. But, if you really want to drink better, then, long before you pick up a corkscrew, you're probably going to have to make some changes to the way you think about wine.

Over the coming pages, you'll find ideas on how to buy wine more effectively. And whether it's trudging up and down the aisles or wading through a wine list, we'll take a more detailed look at how you might improve that experience. I'll explain how to make sense of wine labels. I'll dip into everything from how wine is priced through to how ethics are changing the way we drink. But the real aim of this chapter is to make you a better shopper: to arm you with a little bit of knowledge, confidence, and enthusiasm, which should help take some of the guesswork out of buying wine. Become a better shopper and you're well on your way to becoming the wine-savvy version of you.

Where to shop for wine

As wine drinkers, we live in an age where you can get your hands on just about anything. Our world is no longer confined to a small place and, when it comes to buying wine, the range of experiences available has never been greater.

As someone who buys wine for a living, I can tell you that not all of the buying options on offer will suit everyone, so it's good to have an idea of what you might expect from each one. In this chapter we'll take a closer look at those options, offering you some valuable pointers along the way.

One last thing—at the risk of sounding clichéd, what you put into wine is what you'll get out of it. In other words, if you're looking for safe, dependable, value-for-money drinking with little investment, cash, or otherwise, then that's okay, and it's easily done. But if you're looking to discover new things, expand your repertoire, and increase your chances of drinking more great bottles more often, then you'll need to put as much effort into buying your wine as you would into drinking it.

Buying wine from a supermarket

If you don't mind the fluorescent lighting and the blip-blip of bar code scanners, then supermarkets can be great places to buy wine—provided, that is, you know what you're looking for.

Ever found yourself lost in front of that dizzying wall of bottles, mesmerized—like a rabbit caught in headlights—unable to make a choice simply because there is too much to choose from? It can be a nightmare. That said, there are a number of pluses to buying your wine from a supermarket.

First and foremost, supermarkets have huge buying power, which in turn means better pricing for you and me. If you're on a limited budget and you don't know what you're looking for, then buying your wine from a supermarket will often translate into the best deal for you. The flip side is that what you might make up for in price, you'll probably lose in range and interest. Unless a wine is made in large quantities—we're talking enough to stock and maintain supply to multiple stores—then it's unlikely that a supermarket will stock it. That will exclude almost all but the world's biggest producers right there.

The other major downside is a lack of help at ground level. Very few supermarkets employ designated wine staff to rove the floor and help those of us who are floundering. If shopping for wine at the supermarket is your choice, my advice is do your homework first. Based on what you like, rip wine columns out of magazines and newspapers, search the Internet for reviews—printing the ones you like the sound of—and, most importantly, try to have a decent wine guide with you whenever you're shopping for wine.

> "Supermarkets have huge buying power, which means better pricing for you and me"

The supermarket wine section is generally laid out first by color. There will usually be a designated side for reds and another for whites. Wines are then usually grouped by country of origin and beyond that by variety. It's a simple formula that is geared toward convenience. The assumption is that you'll most probably be in a rush—meter running, baby crying, kids needing to be picked up, dinner in the oven —and will more or less know what you want, if not specifically. Beat the system and be prepared.

Pros of buying wine from a supermarket

• Competitive prices
• Simple layout of the wine department, geared toward convenience

ABOVE A sea of wine and you're on your own. Try reading up beforehand, or take your favorite wine guide with you.

Buying wine from a chain wine store

My first real job in wine was working for a popular chain wine store. I worked at one of the bigger branches, which, as I was junior, meant long hours hauling boxes of wine and beer from one end of the store to the other.

It was backbreaking work, which all but guaranteed I was exhausted at the end of each day.

But, hard as it was, I loved my job. For the first time since I'd accidentally found my way into the wine industry, I had the chance to work with a team of people my own age—most of whom were just as eager to learn about wine as I was. As staff we were lucky enough to work for an employer who valued good employee training.

"The biggest plus of all comes in the form of the staff"

Along with the physical labor, the drunks, the shoplifters, and the penny-pinchers, there were also chances to visit vineyards, meet winemakers from faraway places, help out at wine shows, and, most importantly, taste a huge amount of wine from home and abroad. I loved that job so much that, if you're ever contemplating a sea change into the world of wine, I strongly recommend making a local wine retailer the first stop in your hunt for employment.

Chain wine or liquor stores offer buyers a number of benefits. At street level, they combine the buying power of supermarkets, but with an expanded yet still relatively commercial range. As with supermarkets, wines will generally be laid out by color, country, and then variety. Most of these chain stores will offer significant discounts if you're buying 12 or more bottles, free or discounted delivery, multiple and conveniently located branches, regular tastings and events, and, increasingly, customer loyalty schemes, too.

But the biggest plus of all with these chains comes in the form of the staff, as the one thing that really separates this buying experience from what you might find in your local supermarket is the people. If you know what you're looking for, if price is important, and if knowledgeable service matters to you, then chain wine stores are great places to buy your wine.

Pros of buying wine from a chain wine or liquor store

• Competitive prices
• Good range
• Knowledgeable staff
• Tastings and events

RIGHT Friendly staff will help guide you to what you want. The more information you can give them about what you do and don't like, the better your chances are of ending up with something great.

Buying from an independent wine merchant

Finding a decent wine store is your key to getting more out of wine.

Pros of buying wine from an independent wine merchant

- Good range, including off-the-beaten-track wines
- Knowledgeable staff—often the owner
- Mailing lists and regular tastings

RIGHT Stay ahead by striking up a good relationship with your preferred independent wine merchant; they can personalize your wine choice.

Any good independent wine store will have people who know more than just a little standing behind the counter, which often will mean the owner.

The worst thing that can happen to you in a small independent is that you ask for a recommendation, only to be pointed in the direction of what's selling. But trust me, with so much emphasis being placed on the quality of products in independents, that ain't so bad.

The best-case scenario is a whole lot rosier: namely that your local independent has a team of passionate, enthusiastic, and knowledgeable staff. Better still, you strike up a relationship with one of them—someone who really knows what they're talking about—and so the road to better drinking begins.

Aside from one-on-one service, independent wine merchants can offer range where the bigger players cannot. We're not simply talking about the number of wines stocked; we're talking about a mixture of small-scale, off-the-beaten track, artisan producers alongside low-volume, super-premium classics from those with established and well-earned

reputations. And if the merchant doesn't carry it, then in many cases the staff or owner will bend over backward trying to track it down for you. How wines are displayed will vary from merchant to merchant, but most commonly wines are grouped by variety and/or country.

The more information that you can give your local independent about what you like to drink—including price, variety, country, style, and loves and hates—the closer they're likely to get to finding you something that really matches your taste. From here the trick is letting them lead you. Allow them to show you new things.

The other great advantage to buying wine from an independent wine merchant is that in most cases they'll offer a mailing list, which I'd strongly recommend that you join. Mailing lists are a great way to find out about a range of regular customer events, such as free weekly tastings; if you're looking to expand your drinking repertoire, these offer the perfect opportunity to try before you buy. From small and quirky through to ultra-premium, this is often where you'll find the best combination of hard-to-get products and expert service.

Buying wine from the Internet

Food, books, music, clothes, electrical items. You name it, and you can bet it's for sale on the Net.

Wine retailing on the Internet is still in its infancy. Many have tried, and plenty have failed. Slow deliveries, hidden extras, insecure sites, poor availability, damaged goods, not to mention the occasional bad online retailer—you can't be too careful.

Competitive pricing aside, the pluses include availability of rare and hard-to-get products and door-to-door service.

The minuses—and there are a few—are that, while pricing can look attractive when compared with chain retailers and independents, shipping costs often negate any discounts, there's the ever-present risk of online fraud, and delivery times can be erratic.

So if you do intend to buy wine online, you need to tread with care. Below are some basic guidelines.

Pros of buying wine from the Internet

- Fantastic range
- Availability of mature wines
- Availability of classic wines no longer in the mainstream
- Door-to-door service
- Competitive prices

Tips for online success

1. Buy from a reputable online supplier
The Internet is full of less-than-trustworthy retailers just waiting to take your money. Shop with an established retailer: preferably someone with a physical store as well as an online presence. Online customer feedback is worth checking out, too.

2. Call to check that your order has been received
This is a great way to ensure that not only has the supplier received your order and details, but also that what you ordered is available.

3. Confirm the shipping details
Confirmation of delivery times aside, there are often extra charges that are payable on delivery, so this is the ideal time to double-check exactly what's expected.

4. Make sure that your order is traceable
Check with your online retailer about whether there is an order number and/or tracking number that you can use to monitor the location of your delivery, should it get lost or delayed. Often, you can follow the delivery progress of your order online.

Buying wine at an auction

Auction houses are places of extremes.

On one hand, they offer some of the rarest, most exclusive, and collectable wines in the world, while on the other, they offer the rest of us a chance to pick up mature bargains—everyday wines that, no longer commercially available, are ripe and ready for drinking now.

While some highly collectable wines push the limit and command stratospheric prices at an auction, many wines are offered at 20–30 percent below normal retail prices. I should clarify that auction houses are not in the business of selling wine, but rather reselling it—we largely have death, debt, and divorce to thank for that.

The benefits of buying wine at an auction are great. Auctions offer you the chance to buy mature wine that has, in all but a few cases, been properly cellared and cared for. It's a chance to get your hands on classic wines that are no longer in mainstream circulation, with most high-end collectables increasing at a rate of 5–7 percent per annum, and many doubling their value every decade. They also offer a great opportunity for investment.

The only drawback of wine auctions is that you can't inspect "individual lots" prior to them going under the hammer. But rest assured, nearly all auction houses carry out a thorough and stringent pre-auction assessment on all salable wines, rating them by producer, type, vintage, rarity, and condition.

Pros of buying wine at an auction

- Availability of mature wines
- Availability of classic wines no longer in mainstream circulation
- Good investment opportunities

ABOVE Buying wine at an auction can be a lot of fun and very rewarding. Take advantage of the highly qualified consultants and pre-auction tastings to expand your knowledge.

Tips on buying wine at an auction

1. Start by contacting a reputable auction house

2. Find out what auctions are coming up
Request a list of what's being sold so that you can plan ahead.

3. Arrange to meet an in-house consultant
Most auction houses have in-house consultants who will be happy to advise/work with you, no matter how little you know about wine, in order to help you build a cellar.

4. Ask lots of questions
Similarly, give the consultant as much information as possible about the kind of wines that you like.

5. Do some research
Ask for a copy of the last auction results and check out what sold and for how much.

6. Attend the pre-auction tasting
Although these are mostly prepaid events, this is a great way to not only taste some great old wines, but also to try before you buy. This is also a good chance to meet your in-house consultant to discuss what you do and don't like.

7. On the day of the auction, commit to the whole event
Often many of the best bargains go at the beginning of the day, while people are still getting used to the environment, and also toward the end of the day, with the more exclusive lots having already been sold and the crowd diminishing.

8. Remember that if you can't make the event you can submit absentee bids by phone, fax, or over the Internet.

9. Set yourself a limit and stick to it.

Buying wine in a restaurant

Those of you who order the second-cheapest bottle of wine (and we're talking about more than just a handful of you here)—be it in a bar or restaurant—and think it's the safest and the best-value option, think again.

Tips on buying wine in a restaurant

- Consult the sommelier
- Be as specific as possible with the sommelier about what you like
- Match the wine with your food
- Consider wines served by the glass or half bottle
- Know your budget

RIGHT Turn the scary wine list situation around: be armed by knowing your budget and whether it's the food and wine experience you are after, or just an enjoyable bottle.

We all know that buying wine in a restaurant can be tricky and intimidating and that a wine list you can't navigate can be all it takes to dampen a fun night out. Throw in some good old-fashioned pompous service and you have most people's idea of dining hell. But, come on! Every smart wine buyer in town knows the old "second-cheapest bottle trick," and as a result many less scrupulous buyers price the second-cheapest bottle to be the most profitable one on their list. Promise me that you won't do that again. From now on, I want you to take a new approach to choosing wine. Here's how you do it.

Consult the sommelier
The days of the stereotypical snobby sommelier are well and truly numbered, if not over, so if a restaurant has a sommelier or a wine waiter or waitress, I urge you to use him or her.

Identify styles you like
The more information you can give the sommelier about what wines you do and don't like, the easier it'll be for him or her to pinpoint something great for you to drink. One of my best friends, Paul, an excellent sommelier, thinks that buying wine is like getting a haircut:

if you're not specific about what you want and end up disappointed, you have no one to blame but yourself. Very true—I know just how good that advice is.

Matching wine and food
Start with the food. Give some thought to what you're going to eat and use that as a springboard for choosing your wine. Next, decide whether you're in for the complete food and wine experience or just a bottle of something nice that's not necessarily matched with the food.

Half bottles and wines by the glass
These are worth considering, as both mean that you can vary what you drink without having to drink multiple bottles. But if you are drinking by the glass, make sure that the wine is fresh; you buy wine by the glass based on the assumption that it's in perfect condition. If in doubt, get the sommelier or bar staff to check it.

Your budget
Give the sommelier a budget. This is important, as it allows the sommelier to focus on picking out the best wines in your price range. Often, the best-value wines come from lesser-known regions and varieties, so try something new.

Buying wine from a vineyard

Having grown up a city kid, my imagination for what lay beyond the concrete sprawl was always limited.

Pros of buying wine from a vineyard

• The opportunity to taste the wine, sometimes with the person who made it
• Supporting the producer
• Value for money

RIGHT Seeing in person how wine is actually made will do more to develop your understanding and knowledge of wine than anything else—get out there and get inspired.

So when I began working in the wine industry, the possibility that I might one day be visiting vineyards wasn't significant to me. I worked in a store where we sold bottles of wine. I knew they came from somewhere—I just never really gave the "where" much consideration. And then an invitation came to visit a small producer northeast of Melbourne, Australia. My first-ever trip to a winery. The day before the visit, I remember wondering what I'd be likely to see. To start with, I pictured a large gray factory, complete with smoking chimneys, barbed-wire fences, CCTV, and a large parking lot. Inside, there would be lots of people in white lab coats and protective clothing, and I imagined that, aside from the humming of machines, it would all be pretty quiet and hospital-like. There would be lots of gleaming stainless steel, and, being visitors from the city, we'd probably be led around in hard hats by a guide. Maybe my picture was a little extreme, but hopefully you know what I'm getting at . . .

If you've never done so before, please visit a vineyard. Hopefully, you'll discover that vineyards are farms—farms that are completely exposed to the elements—and that growing grapes, really top-quality grapes, takes far more effort than you might ever have considered. You'll also see how logical the process of grape growing and winemaking is, despite the challenges from Mother Nature.

" . . . you also stand to save money from buying direct"

Depending on where you go, you'll realize that very few wineries actually resemble what I'd first imagined. Most of all, I hope you'll realize that tasting wine with the person who made it, in the place where it was made, right next to the place where the grapes grew, is a unique experience that is impossible to reproduce. From my experience, wine rarely tastes better than at the place where it was made.

There are several pluses to buying your wine at a winery. Aside from the fact that you are directly supporting the producer, which in many cases will be the same person that grew the grapes and made the wine, you also stand to save money from buying direct. You'll save on taxes, you'll save on transportation, if you are lucky enough to live within day-trip distance of a good winery or two—although it will probably cost you a tank of gas and a nice lunch—and if you do purchase wine, you'll do so knowing it's been correctly stored. You'll also have fun, and probably end up learning more about wine in a few hours than you've ever learned before.

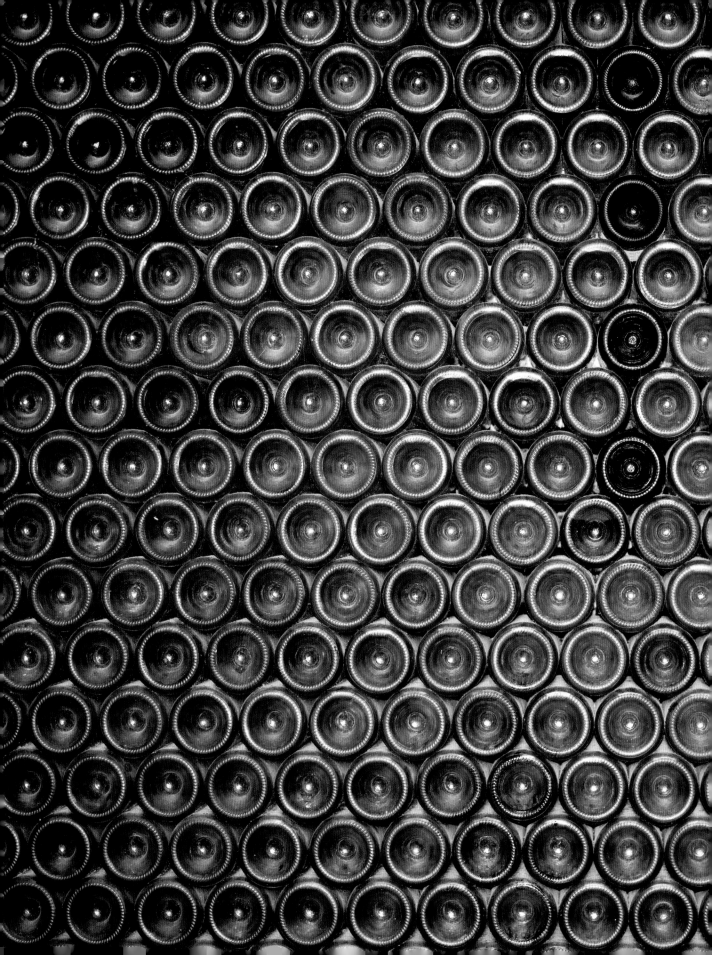

The bottle: facts and fiction

Along with the rumor that goth rocker Marilyn Manson played the geeky but lovable Paul Pfeiffer in the TV series *The Wonder Years*, another of my favorite urban myths is the one regarding KISS bass player Gene Simmons. Apparently Simmons, in order to enhance his demonlike onstage persona, had a cow's tongue grafted onto his own. How ridiculous. Run that past any self-respecting oral surgeon, butcher, or the man himself, and they'll probably dismiss that one as the work of bored ten-year-olds. Although nowhere near as gruesome, the world of wine is not without the occasional tall tale, especially when it comes to theories on how to choose good bottles of wine. I think I've heard them all: the higher the alcohol content; the heavier the bottle; the darker the glass; the prettier the label; even the supposed importance of the depth of the indentation in a bottle's base—all are rumored to signify a better wine. If only it were that simple. Although, with one quarter of you making your choice on label design and nearly one third of you basing your decision on alcoholic strength, sometimes fact is stranger than fiction.

The truth is that there are many factors that determine quality, and, while country, region, and variety all play vital roles, no detail is quite as important as the reputation of the wine's producer. Starting off with how to read a wine label correctly, here are a few things to keep an eye out for.

How to make sense of a wine label

A wine label is little bit like a passport. It tells you what it is, who it's from, what it's from, when it's from, and where it's from, too.

Distilling the information contained on a wine label can be trickier than trying to solve a Rubik's Cube without removing the stickers, but there are a number of important pieces of information contained on a wine label that will help you better evaluate what's inside the bottle. Below, in order of priority, is a list of key points worth considering the next time you pick up a bottle of wine.

Producer

This is the most important piece of information contained on any label, no matter where in the world the wine has come from. The reputation of the producer counts for everything. Understanding who the better producers are is the difference between good wine and great wine.

Variety

This all depends on where your wine originates from. If your bottle hails from the New World—meaning Australia, New Zealand, South Africa, Argentina, Chile, Uruguay, and the U.S.—chances are it will be labeled by variety, in which case you can proceed directly to the next step. But if your wine happens to come from the Old World—and that's Europe—it will more than likely be labeled by region. This system assumes that you already know what grapes are permitted by law to be grown within a particular region—a fairly big assumption considering what most of us really know about wine.

Region and vineyard

Some varieties are better suited to specific spots on the planet, and within those areas you'll often find that there are certain sites (also know as vineyards) from which the best examples come. It might be climate, it might be soil, it might be altitude—it might be a mixture of all three—but as you become more familiar with wine, understanding how particular regions, and beyond that vineyards, influence varieties will almost certainly influence how you choose your wine.

Key   >>

1 Producer

2 Variety

3 Region and vineyard

4 Vintage

5 Alcohol

Vintage

The year that appears on the label refers to the year in which the grapes were harvested. This is referred to as the "vintage." It's really important to remember that no two years—even in the same spot—will ever be the same. That's the beauty of Mother Nature. No matter what you do, you can't control the elements.

As a result, some vintages are better than others. In order to know which are the better years, you'll need to do a bit of reading, invest in a decent wine guide, or get some expert advice.

> "A pretty label is a great way to sell an ordinary bottle of wine, while back labels will never tell you how 'bad' a wine is"

Alcohol

Alcoholic volume is measured as a percentage and found on the bottom of either the front or back labels. While this is a compulsory requirement, it's important to keep in mind that alcoholic strength has no bearing on quality.

There is no minimum amount of alcohol required for wine to qualify as "wine." Once a wine hits 16 percent ABV however, you're quickly heading into fortified territory.

Additives

While all but a few wines contain additives used at various stages during their production, only some countries require that they be recorded on the label. The most common additives in wine are preservatives such as sulfur dioxide—an antioxidant that is often listed as 221 or 225—while other additives such as fining agents (for taking any impurities out of the wine prior to bottling) produced from egg or fish solutions are simply recorded by a line, usually on the back, stating, "This wine is not suitable for vegetarians/vegans."

A few things to be wary of

If you don't know a huge amount about wine, then it's very easy to be lead by aesthetics. A pretty label is a great way to sell an ordinary bottle of wine, while back labels will never tell you how "bad" a wine is. While a stylish label isn't necessarily covering for a bad or ordinary wine, it shouldn't be taken as an automatic indicator of quality. A label is just that—a label.

The application of gold medals to bottles is also another great way of making an average wine stand out in a crowd. While some medals are warranted, due to the reputation of the competition in which they were judged, others are not, and it's important to remember that not all wine shows are held with equal regard. For this reason, make sure you do your homework on which wine shows are worth following.

Why are some bottles bigger than others?

It's really important to remember that, while the size of a bottle has no bearing on the quality of the contents inside, it will determine how a wine will develop over time.

It all comes down to a little matter of oxygen versus liquid. While big bottles contain a greater volume of liquid, comparatively they have a smaller amount of oxygen than your standard (750ml) bottle of wine. So what does that mean?

Well, wine is a living, breathing liquid that we generally consume somewhere on its journey from grape juice to vinegar. Contact with oxygen will help speed up that journey. And so to that end bigger bottles will generally mean slower and more gradual aging, while smaller bottles (with a greater oxygen/wine ratio) will develop far more quickly—an ideal situation if you're impatient!

A note on bottle shape
There are three major shapes of bottle: Bordeaux (high shoulder), Champagne and Burgundy (sloped shoulder), and Germany (tall and thin). Generally, the wine from the grapes of these regions will be bottled in the corresponding bottle shape, regardless of where the wine is made. But the larger bottle shapes hold different quantities, and so there is plenty of argument as to what different-size bottles should be called. However, using the Champagne and Burgundy table, below are the most common bottle sizes available.

BELOW The size and shape of bottles are important for aging but can be confusing when judging quantity. Most of the names are simply biblical and of no great significance.

½ bottle (375ml) Half bottle

1 bottle (750ml) Standard bottle

2 bottles (1.5L) Magnum

4 bottles (3L) Jeroboam

6 bottles (4.5L) Rehoboam

8 bottles (6L) Methuselah

12 bottles (9L) Salmanazar

16 bottles (12L) Balthazar

20 bottles (15L) Nebuchadnezzar

Where have all the corks gone?

When was the last time you opened a bottle of wine sealed with a cork? I'm not talking about one of those hernia-inducing plastic replicas; I'm talking about the real deal—an actual cork.

Why some wine is corked

• Strain on the cork industry caused by the ever-increasing popularity of wine has resulted in production standards not having been up to par for some time.

• In particular, cork is susceptible to a type of naturally occurring fungi that results in a chemical compound known as 2,4,6-trichloroanisole (TCA for short) that can contaminate cork during production. Right now it's estimated that somewhere between 5–7 percent of all wines bottled under a conventional cork ends up being affected by TCA.

• This is not pieces of cork floating in the wine—caused by a bad cork-screw—but shows up as a damp, musty, wet cardboard aroma.

• Although not harmful to us, this strips the wine of all its beautiful aroma and flavor. This is what we call "cork-tainted wine."

• At worst, "cork taint" stands out like a pink T-shirt at a Metallica concert, but it's when the taint is really slight, when it's barely detectable, when even those of us who work with wine struggle to spot it, that TCA becomes every winemaker's worst nightmare.

Chances are it was some time ago. Nowadays we have rubber plugs, glass stoppers, aluminum screw caps, tin lids, and those awful plastic replicas. But where have all the real corks gone?

Corks have natural spring and high density, they're strong, and they're semipermeable yet near impenetrable. For the better part of the past 150 years, cork has been the wine industry's commercial closure of choice. And for good reason, too.

As a wine ages, cork allows a slow, constant flow of oxygen into the bottle, which can have an amazing effect on some wines— but not all. That corks come from sustainable sources and can be recycled makes them just about perfect. Just about . . .

The big fear is that you buy a bottle of corked wine, you open it—it's ever so slightly corked (see box, left), but you don't notice—you drink it, you don't especially like it, and as a result you decide not to buy that wine again. That's what winemakers really fear. And so in order to eliminate that scenario, many winemakers have started looking for alternatives.

Here enters our motley range of materials. It's fair to say that the wine industry hasn't completely given up on corks—nor has it given up on looking for good alternatives. Do some research and make up your own mind as to which closure you prefer, but, whatever you decide, please promise me you won't be influenced by aesthetics, preconceptions, or out-of-date traditions.

In 2006 the U.K.-based International Wine Challenge announced that of the 13,477 wines tasted, 7.2 percent —or 1 in 14 bottles—was faulty. Almost half of the faulty wines had problems that could be traced back to the closure, with cork taint accounting for around 28 percent of faults, oxidation due to imperfect seals almost 17 percent, and faulty screw caps 5 percent.

RIGHT Cork continues to be the preferred closure for wine, and this is mostly down to consumer demand. Alternative closures are still perceived as cheap.

Alternatives to cork

Screw caps, crown seals, synthetic corks, glass tops, twin tips, composites—the increase of cork-tainted wine has produced a flood of alternatives.

To date, screw caps have proven to be the most successful alternative to cork, although early signs indicate that glass tops and cork-based technical closures such as DIAM look like worthy contenders. Here's a brief rundown of what is available and how they differ.

Agglomerates
Agglomerate corks are made up of lots of little chopped-up pieces of cork (of varying quality) that are bound together with glue and reassembled in the shape of a cork. They are often smaller than a regular cork, which allows the manufacturer to produce more of them. Agglomerates also vary dramatically in quality due to the sheer volume of producers turning them out. Unfortunately, the fact that these are still produced from cork—often from low-grade material—means that cork taint is still a problem.

Key ‹‹
1. Cork
2. Screw cap
3. DIAM cork
4. Agglomerate
5. Synthetic closure
6. Vino-seal glass stopper

Synthetic closures
Synthetic closures are produced from plastic compounds. Dismissed from many corners of the wine industry, synthetic closures are not only difficult to remove, but also harder to reapply to an open bottle. The other main problem is that synthetic closures don't have the spring of a natural cork, which means that, if the inside of your bottle contains any imperfections, you run the risk of random oxidation—in other words, air coming into contact with your wine. Synthetic corks have also been linked to "plastic taint."

Crown seal
As the closure of choice for beers far and wide, crown seals have also been used for many moons in the production of sparkling wine and Champagne. But by the time Champagne bottles get to us, crown seals have been removed and replaced by a cork. Made from recycled aluminum and containing a silicon liner, crown seals prevent the wine from TCA contamination and the risk of oxidation, but they cannot be reapplied to the bottle once removed.

Vino-seal
A vino-seal is a glass stopper-like closure with a silicon ring that was developed in 2003. Early signs show that it is as effective as the screw cap in preventing spoilage from TCA and random oxidation.

For those of you who still struggle to get your heads around screw caps, Vino-seal is a great alternative. It is also easily reapplied to an open bottle of wine. In fact, the only real downside at present is the cost of production, which right now is about twice that of a screw cap.

Stelvin closure/screw cap
Screw caps are a tin or aluminum-based closure lined with a silicon membrane that forms an airtight seal between the closure and the bottle. Aside from being highly effective in combating against TCA and oxidation, screw caps also help preserve aromatic freshness and prolong a wine's aging potential. A screw cap costs about the same to produce as a high-grade cork, but its downside remains the lingering cheap image that was associated with many poorer screw capped wines from decades ago. (See also page 43.)

DIAM
DIAM is a high-tech, cork-based closure made up of cork granules treated under the DIAMANT process—a form of CO_2 saturation that has also been used to decaffeinate coffee. The process not only extracts TCA but also more than 150 other negative compounds. With many of the world's great producers currently trailing, and in some cases using DIAM, the early research findings are very positive.

Why your favorite wine now has a screw cap

Do you remember racing off on your bike with your mom or dad in hot pursuit, shouting at you to come back and put on your helmet?

And you know what, it probably wouldn't have been so bad, except for the fact that my helmet was twice the size of my head, bright orange, and called a "stackhat"— an excellent lifesaver maybe, but not so excellent for a 13-year-old's street cred . . .

Anyway, as you've probably noticed, screw caps are big news. And just like my big orange stackhat, they're not especially pretty. But screw caps do exist for a couple of really good reasons, and you should know why.

In a nutshell, it's estimated that somewhere around 5 percent of all wine bottled with a traditional cork ends up being affected by cork taint (see page 38). The other big problem is random oxidation— the random and premature aging of a wine due to prolonged oxygen exposure—a problem that is much harder to measure than cork taint.

So what's the solution, then?

Winemakers are desperate and have explored nearly every possible avenue in a bid to identify something better than a cork. Enter the screw cap. Romantic they're not, but they do guarantee that 99.9 percent of the time your wine will taste as the winemaker intended. They slow the aging process, which is beneficial in aging wines. And they are easy to

open and close without the need for lots of wine accessories. Surely that's a good thing?

Well, there are some sticking points. Currently, there is some debate about the possibility of wines under a screw cap giving off a "reduced" smell when first opened. This can occur because of a lack of oxygen in the bottle due to the effectiveness of the seal. This smell diffuses, however, once the wine has been opened and poured.

> "Romantic they're not, but they do guarantee that 99.9 percent of the time your wine will taste as the winemaker intended"

And, while most of the wine-loving southern hemisphere has embraced screw caps with open arms (as much as 92 percent of New Zealand's entire production is now under a screw cap), the sad fact is that poor consumer perception in some of the world's more conservative, yet financially important, markets has convinced many Old World producers to stick with cork for the time being. Time will tell.

LEFT AND ABOVE With more pros than cons, the screw cap should be celebrated for its ease of opening and for keeping our wine super fresh.

The wine: facts and fiction

First and foremost, there is no easy way to learn about wine. If you want to drink better, you're going to have to taste more and think more —step outside your comfort zone and open your mind to trying new things. Think about the price of wine and how it breaks down, know the difference between Old World and New World, consider organic, biodynamic, or Fairtrade wines.

There is no trick to choosing great bottles, just knowledge—although there is still a lot of myth surrounding how you measure quality.

Also know that special offers are rarely all that special: as with most things in life, with wine you pretty much get what you pay for.

Finally, never forget that while learning more about wine will undoubtedly help, you don't need to know a huge amount in order to simply drink better. The following pages give an insight into the considerations involved in producing wine, allowing you to shop smarter.

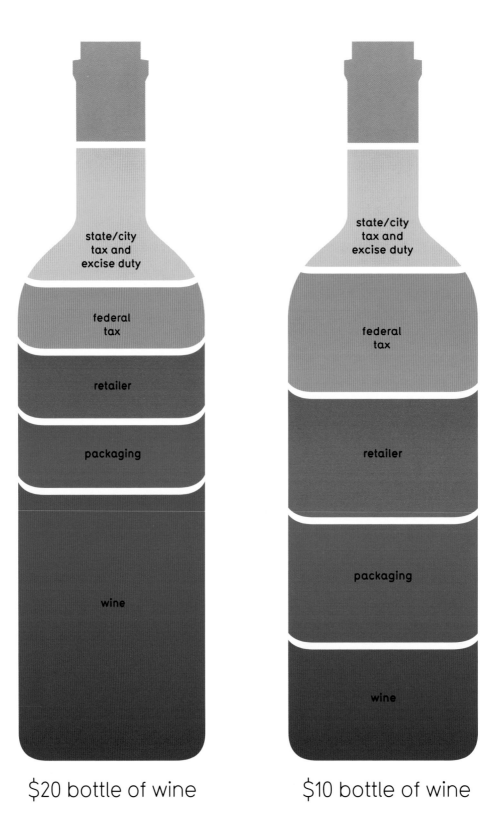

state/city
tax and
excise duty

federal
tax

retailer

packaging

wine

$20 bottle of wine

state/city
tax and
excise duty

federal
tax

retailer

packaging

wine

$10 bottle of wine

What makes one bottle more expensive than another?

What a tricky question. How long is a piece of string? I am probably asked this question more than any other, and to be honest, the answer isn't quite as straightforward as you might hope.

Besides considering what the wine is, the answer requires you to think about everything, from where and when it was made through to who made it, how they made it, and how much of it was made. There's a lot to think about as there are many contributing factors that end up determining a wine's price. Think cars for a minute, there are cars, and then there are cars. Price varies dramatically depending on what it is, where it's from, who made it etc. See what I'm saying?

When it comes down to where your money goes, in the U.S. this is a tricky business. There are taxes and duties levied at the Federal level and then at the state level. The Federal 'Gallonage Tax' is levied on gallons produced or imported, using a rate scale based on the alcohol content of the wine. For the purpose of this book we'll consider wines under 14% alcohol, that receive $1.07/gallon. There are tax credits available for domestic producers producing under 250,000 gallons of wine per year, but these are also on a sliding scale depending on 'gallonage' and so it is best to visit www.ttb.gov for further details.

On state level there are often (but not always) two taxes comprising a state tax and a city or county tax. These two can be averaged and range between no taxes levied and 9.4%. There is then state excise duty that also varies by state but generally ranges between $0.2–2.5/gallon, although there are other chargeable conditions for some states. There are also tax/duty credits for domestic producers at this level.

But, what you need to know is that by the time the salesman has added his mark-up then there is a hard and fast rule to remember – the difference in quality between a $10 and $15 wine is surprisingly high once all the costs are added to the initial cost of the wine.

What influences the price of a bottle

1. Where wine comes from
As the price of a wine increases, so do the number of factors that make up the price. Production costs vary greatly, so where in the world your wine comes from is the first contributing factor to the end price.

2. Producer and perceived quality
Established and well-earned reputations come at a price, so who made your wine plays a significant role. But some producers without reputation will price their wines based on the reputation of the region, its benchmarks, the variety, and the perceived value of their brand.

3. Grape varieties
While some grape varieties seem to be resistant to fashion, plenty are not, and prices are driven up or down accordingly.

4. Vintage
While the best producers will make great wines even in the trickiest of years, the quality of the year will play its part, too—although ironically, even in the worst years, wines rarely ever go down in price, with Bordeaux perhaps being the one exception.

5. Rarity
If there's less of it, and there's demand, then the price will go up.

6. Age
Similarly, as a rare wine gets older, the number of bottles left in circulation will have a significant impact on the price of the wine.

What makes a good year

Essentially, the difference between good years and bad years comes down to Mother Nature.

To start with, I should clarify what I mean by "year." The year (or vintage, as it's known in the wine world) that appears on a bottle of wine refers to the year in which the grapes were harvested.

> "The appearance of a vintage acts as a valuable reference point for knowing when the perfect time to drink your wine is"

Few wines appear without a vintage on the label; exceptions to the rule include Champagne, port, and sherry, where, even though single vintage examples are produced, often wines are created by blending a number of different years in order to maintain a consistent house style year in, year out.

Climate is the real key. Grapes are delicate creatures—they like long, dry growing seasons; they like sun; and a little bit of water, although not too much; and they like it warm. Aside from a lack of warmth, or too much warmth, the real threat to vineyards comes during the springtime, when frosts are prone to literally freezing new growth from vines. Assuming the vines make it through the spring, the summer also brings with it the threat of rain and hail—both of which can completely ruin a crop of grapes.

Beyond that, other factors that help determine a good year might include how the vineyards were managed and/or how the wine was handled in the winery. To this end the appearance of a vintage also acts as a valuable reference point for knowing when the perfect time to drink your wine is.

LEFT The only real variable affecting the vintage is weather, which is why it is a good idea to keep an eye on vintage reports for your favorite wine areas.

What vintages to try

Vintage is important in any wine-buying decision, especially if you are splashing out for a special occasion or if you are in a restaurant. In this situation, use the knowledge of the person selling you the wine.

If you have a cellar and you want to know when to drink a wine, then refer to magazines or books on the subject. Below I've recommended vintages by country or region (but there will be variation within country).

California		Washington	Oregon	Bordeaux		Burgundy		Champagne	Germany		Italy	Spain
Red	White			Red	White	Red	White					
2005	2005	2005	2002	2005	2005	2005	2005	2004	2005	1997	2005	2005
2003	2004	2001	1999	2000	2001	1999	2000	2002	2003	1996	2004	2004
2002	1997	1989	1994	1995	1999	1995	1997	2000	2001	1995	1999	2001
2001	1995			1990	1996		1996	1999	1999	1994	1997	1995
1997	1992			1989	1990		1995	1996	1998		1996	1994
1994					1989			1995				
1990												

New World vs. Old World

So what are New World and Old World wines anyway, and what are the differences between them?

Marketing wine

In just 20 years, the New World has largely seduced wine lovers everywhere. It's done so in almost Pied Piper-like fashion through:
• clean and well-made wines
• straight-talking labels
• intelligent branding
• even more intelligent marketing.
It's allowed producers to escape the regional red tape that governs the production and labeling of many European wines, while for the consumer it's largely signalled the democratization of wine.

RIGHT No matter which style you prefer, it is worth remembering that nowadays the flow of information and experience between the Old World and the New World is bringing them closer together.

First things first: when it comes to wine, the New World refers to the wine-producing countries of Australia, New Zealand, South Africa, Chile, Argentina, Uruguay, and the U.S., while the Old World encompasses all of winemaking Europe. But the differences that split them go way beyond where they sit on the globe.

"It's a clash of attitudes, but essentially we're talking about technology versus tradition"

While the New World has been creating wines that are clean and precise, and speak very clearly of their grape variety, much of the Old World remains on a mission to highlight the opposite. In fact, the Old World would argue that, long before variety, the most important character for any wine to exhibit is the character of where it is from.

The French have a word for it, *terroir*. It has no straightforward English translation but describes the personality of a wine due to the many different environmental factors that have affected its production: the sun, the soil, the water, the wildlife, the everything.

It's a clash of attitudes, but essentially we're talking about technology versus tradition. And who's right? Who knows. Perhaps a decade ago that would have been a far easier question to answer, but the modern world of wine can be a very tricky place.

Once both heavily and easily defined, the lines between the Old World and the New World are becoming more and more blurred. As the new generation of winemakers comes home to their estates or châteaus after flying around the world working vintages in foreign climes, they bring back with them experiences, ideas, and new attitudes. The Old World is picking up tricks from the New World in order to clean up its wines, while the New World is busy trying to force more regional influence into the bottle.

This means we, the consumers, win out from a meeting of wine minds—a merging of these two worlds—and a new range of wine styles from old favorites.

"Once both heavily and easily defined, the lines are becoming more and more blurred"

About organic wine

And then, just to make things that little bit more complicated, environmental and ethical issues have entered the wine arena. You should know about them, as these issues not only affect production, but go a long way toward helping entire communities and the environment, too.

Environmental and ethical issues will undoubtedly influence how you buy wine in years to come. Here's a brief summary.

Once a word you simply filed between "bean sprouts" and "yoga", "organic" has infiltrated all things consumable, wine included, and has quickly become a mainstream way of life. By definition, organic wines are those produced from grapes grown without the use of industrial fertilizers, herbicides, fungicides, pesticides, and excluding the addition of synthetic additives—basically all the nasty stuff.

Given our rising curiosity for knowing more about what we eat and drink, organic farming is a natural and responsible practice through which many of the world's greatest wines are, and have long been, produced. The growing number of great-value examples hitting shelves everywhere is all the more encouraging.

For a producer to be certified as organic they have to meet a specific list of criteria relating to how they grow their grapes and how they make their wine. It's worth remembering that there are many producers who have long practiced organic or biodynamic viticulture, but who pull up short of certification.

It's a safe option that allows you to be organic right up to the point where things go horribly wrong, at which time you may intervene. And while each country has its own criteria for organic certification, there are several practices that are common to all throughout the world of organic wine production.

"The growing number of great-value organic wines hitting shelves everywhere is all the more encouraging"

To start with, grapes must be grown without the use of chemical fertilizers, herbicides, pesticides, and fungicides. Once the grapes arrive at the winery, limited manipulation of the wine is permitted; this excludes the practices of reverse osmosis (the process of separating solvents such as smoke taint, Brettanomyces, volatile acidity, and excessive alcohol from the main body of wine), excessive filtering of the wine, and the use of flavor additives, such as oak chips. Many organic winemakers also prefer to incorporate wild yeasts (natural yeasts that live within the winery environment) into cultured yeasts (those which are commercially developed for the production of wine) for fermentation. The most contentious issue, though, is the use of sulfur dioxide—a synthetic additive that helps stabilize wine during production. You see, if you want your wine to stay in good condition, even minimal use of sulfur dioxide is required.

The addition of synthetic additives is a big "nono" in the world of organics however, and as a result has spawned an entire generation of "organically minded" producers —those who do everything by the book, but without certification.

LEFT In this day and age, we should hope to see more organic wine from organic vineyards, such as this one, hitting the shelves. It tends to come from smaller producers rather than big brand names, so keep your eye on the labels.

About biodynamic wine

Complex, somewhat unconventional, and highly controversial, biodynamic farming is the brainchild of German philosopher Rudolph Steiner.

ABOVE Interestingly, in reported "tasteoffs" between biodynamic and conventional wines conducted by some of the most influential wine merchants in the world, the biodynamic wines win in every category. Good news all around—drink well and keep you and the world as healthy as possible.

Steiner was primarily concerned with bridging the gap between the material and the physical and, toward the end of his life, applied his spiritual science of anthroposophy to agriculture.

Biodynamics takes organic grape growing (a prerequisite to biodynamic farming) to the next level, and in some cases—depending on how you look at it—to the extreme. In short, it's a way of thinking before it's a way of farming.

> "The list of practicing biodynamic producers reads like a roll call of the wine world's greatest names"

Where organic growing prohibits the use of both chemicals and synthetic additives, biodynamic agriculture takes basic organics and adds elements of homeopathy, astronomy, and astrology.

Rather than simply looking at how to coax the best out of the vines, biodynamics looks at not only the vineyard, but also the entire farm and everything in it as a single living organism. A self-sustaining

entity, which, when cultivated via the application of a number of preparations or manures, operates in line with lunar and cosmic rhythms. This is not as crazy as it might sound at first. Lots of cultures over the years have planted their crops and harvested their produce following the lunar cycle.

Confused? Impressed? Bewildered? Scared? Relax, you wouldn't be alone. Measuring the success of biodynamics isn't easy to do—an exact science it's not—although if you ever needed reassuring that the concept was worthwhile and more than just a passing fad, you'll be happy to know that the list of practicing biodynamic producers reads like a roll call of the wine world's greatest names. Producers that, despite all manner of differences, unanimously agree that biodynamic farming not only improves the health, disease resistance, and longevity of their vines, but also increases the sugar levels within their fruit without a loss in valuable acidity. Watch this space.

About Fairtrade and carbon-neutral wine

The planet is suffering and, as industry slowly faces up to its responsibilities, the wine world is set to get greener by the second.

Beyond wine's green credentials, there are other key ethical issues that are regarded with equal importance. Fairtrade is one of them.

Fairtrade wine

Fairtrade was set up in order to guarantee that disadvantaged producers in the developing world were getting a better deal. Fairtrade products carry a symbol that can be applied only to products that have met criteria set out by Fairtrade standards. These standards cover issues such as paying prices to cover sustainable farming, paying premiums for community development, and committing to partnerships that allow for long-term planning and sustainable production. Currently, Fairtrade wine is available from producers in Argentina, Chile, and South Africa.

> "Many producers are already recycling as much as 80 per cent of their packaging"

Carbon-neutral wine

This is a category coming soon to a wine section near you! At present, the wine industry is looking at a number of ways it can save on energy and reduce the size of its carbon footprint. At ground level, there is an increase in the number of energy-efficient wineries, many of which now include waste-water treatment plants.

There are plans afoot to ship more wine in bulk with a view to bottling closer to the point of sale, thus reducing the amount of energy used during the shipping process. Another initiative will see lighter glass and the introduction of PET plastic bottles, which all together could reduce emissions by as much as 35 percent. Many producers are already recycling as much as 80 percent of their packaging.

Why should we care?

There's a definite air of skepticism toward what's motivating producers to go ethical and environmental. Do they really care, or is it simply an opportunity too good to miss? Should we care?

Even if they are motivated by increased sales, considering the sheer effort required in simply becoming organic—let alone meeting the strict Fairtrade criteria, going biodynamic, or becoming carbon-neutral—then ultimately both the environment and the disadvantaged farmers of the developing world are the winners.

And the really good news is that there are plenty of winemakers out there who are doing it for all the right reasons.

Drinking

Love what you drink

On average, we chew our food nine times before we swallow it. We're supposed to do it 18 times. At roughly one second per chew, that's a whole nine seconds per mouthful of food. Not bad. After all, nine seconds is a fair amount of time—and more than enough to really taste what it is you're eating.

Drinking is a different story. Think about it. You raise a glass to your lips, pour the contents into your mouth, and swallow: into your mouth, over your tongue, down your throat, gone. I wonder how many food products, aside from wine, you regularly purchase that take two to three years to produce? Not many, I suspect. Two to three years in the making; swallowed in a second.

I want you to care about the wine you drink. Not just because of the effort required to produce it, but because of what it costs you. The simple truth is that proportionately, over the course of your lifetime, you may end up spending almost as much on wine as you will on food, so why shouldn't you get every last drop of value out of it?

I want you to start by getting yourself some decent wine glasses: no fancy colors, shapes, or designs— just straightforward glasses. This is going to make a huge difference.

I want you to dig out the decanter you were given as a present and I want you to use it. I want you to get your hands on a decent corkscrew— beg, borrow, or steal it—and, as ridiculous as it may sound, I want you to learn how to open a bottle of wine correctly. But that's not all. I also want you to look at the wine in the glass, smell it, swirl it, and smell it again. I want you to raise the glass to your lips, pour it into your mouth, and hold it there—maybe not for nine seconds, but hold it, swish it around your mouth, get some air into it and really taste it. And once you've done all that, then, only then, can you swallow. Now I want you to do it over and over again. You see, I don't just want you to know that you like what you're drinking. That's not enough. I want you to know what you like about it and why. Wine is a great drink made better with a little consideration, and I want you to care about it because ultimately you want to do so.

Serving wine

If I've learned anything at all about wine—and I've spent many years serving it —it's that great bottles are rarely just about what's inside. They are more often the result of a wider experience, such as who you were with when you drank it, where you were, and what you were eating.

And then there are the little things that, when combined, make a massive difference. Things such as how the wine has been stored, how it is served, at what temperature, and in what kind of glassware. And this applies to drinking wine at home or in a bar or restaurant —so never be afraid to ask or comment on this. Geeky, I know, but trust me when I tell you that it matters.

Next, to help you get the most out of your wine, you're going to have to do a little accessorizing. Here's a rundown of the essentials you'll need to get hold of before we get started.

To start with, you need a decent corkscrew

Once upon a time, a corkscrew was a simple gadget used to pull corks from bottles. No rocket science—just a no-nonsense gadget that was all about function and nothing to do with form.

Today, corkscrews are far more complicated. Admittedly, they perform the same basic function as they did 100 years ago, but now we borrow technology from NASA to build them, we size them so that you'll need a shoulder holster to match, and it almost goes without saying that most come with a list of instructions as long as your arm. Why? Consider where and how often you'll be using it. I'm not going to waste valuable words by going into all the different types of corkscrews and how they work— I'm pretty sure most of you have used one before.

But as I pull corks out of bottles for a living, I can't stress just how important it is to have a decent corkscrew. Not an expensive one, just a decent one. I've lost, broken,

worn out, and snapped more corkscrews than I possibly care to remember. For these reasons, go basic, but not too cheap.

Consider where and how often you'll be using it. If you work in the wine industry or in hospitality,

aim to find something durable, lightweight, compact, and—from experience—that you won't be too disappointed losing. But no matter what style you end up going for and how much you spend, make sure that it at least meets the basic criteria listed in the box below.

What you need from a corkscrew

1. Function
It might look cool, but unless it's easy to use, what's the point?

2. Strength
A corkscrew must be strong enough to withstand a decent amount of pressure. Those made from weak materials often snap or fracture with repeated use.

3. Durability
Before you buy your corkscrew, check that all the joints, hinges, and foil cutter move easily, are not loose, and are in good working order.

4. Action
Is levering the cork from the bottle difficult? Many of the traditional waiter's friend style openers now come with a two-stage lever action that is not only far safer, but also much easier on your wrist.

5. Movement
A lot of corkscrews now have Teflon coating, which reduces the friction between the cork and the screw. Whatever you buy, ensure that the screw has a sharp point—blunt corkscrews will split corks.

6. Extras
Most openers have a foil cutter that's tucked up at one end. Make sure yours has one—serrated blades are great for everyday use.

Key   «

1 Screwpull lever model

2 Traditional corkscrew

3 Winged corkscrew

4 Waiter's friend

Glassware

Forget the pewter goblets—if you're investing time and money in buying better wine, the least you can do is to get some decent glasses to drink it from.

It's like going from a portable black-and-white TV to a wall-mounted 42-inch wide-screen, full-color HDTV model—you're going to be amazed by the difference.

Just like corkscrews, wineglasses come in all shapes and sizes, ranging from cheap and good to ridiculously expensive. Variety, country, region, style—you name it, and you can all but bet there's a glass that's been designed and produced around it. It borders on insanity.

At home I use three different types of wineglasses: a Champagne flute, an all-purpose wineglass,

and a slightly bigger version of that for heavier reds. I can tell you, three is plenty. And while you don't have to spend a fortune on decent wineglasses, you do need to be aware of a few things when you're shopping.

To start with, you want a clear glass—no fancy patterns, colors, or materials—just plain and simple so that you can see the contents within. Secondly, your glass needs a stem. And while this might contradict the current popularity of the stem-free wineglass, it means that you'll keep your hands off the bowl of the glass, which in turn means that you won't risk altering the temperature of your wine.

Shape is also important; while glass size varies dramatically, nearly all wineglasses will have a wider base that tapers toward the rim of the glass. This is to help capture aroma. Lastly, with all that in mind, the materials from which your glass is made (soda lime or lead crystal) and how it was made (by hand, machine, or a mixture of both) will have a huge bearing on what you end up paying for it.

Finally, once you've bought yourself some decent wineglasses, look after them. Dishwashing is fine; otherwise, handwash them in hot, soapy water—not commercial dishwashing soap, which usually has a really strong smell.

"At home I use three different types of wineglasses: a Champagne flute, an all-purpose wineglass, and a slightly bigger version of that for heavier reds"

If handwashing, rinse them under cold water immediately to avoid streaking. Let your glasses dry upsidedown before polishing them with a heavy cotton or linen glass cloth. A fresh towel will be fine, just as long as it's clean. Keep your glasses upright and preferably in a cupboard. You want to try to avoid them picking up aromas from the kitchen or getting overly dusty.

Key «

1 Sparkling

2 Light red or full bodied white

3 Light delicate white

4 Full bodied red

5 Champagne

6 Sweet

7 Fortified

Decanters

There's no end to the range of wine paraphernalia available to you, but if you're going to invest in just one accessory, please make it a decanter.

Every home should have one. Wine is a living, breathing thing that we consume somewhere on its journey from grape juice to vinegar, and the fact that it's been cooped up inside a bottle for an extended period of time will probably mean that it'll need a blast of fresh air when you eventually pull the cork, twist the cap, or remove the stopper. It's just like going on a long journey in the car: in order to feel better, the first thing you do when you arrive is stretch your legs. Decanters help wine to stretch, or breathe.

Although most wines available for stores have been produced with the knowledge that they're unlikely to see the inside of a cellar, they'll still benefit—red or white—from a quick run through a decanter 15 minutes before you plan on serving them. This will not only help soften the wine, but it will also help to shake off any unpleasant aromas (faults aside) that may have been picked up in the bottle.

Decanters serve two main purposes: they allow wine to breathe and they're also especially handy when it comes to removing sediment and other floating nasties from older wines. Decanting to remove sediment may require you to transfer the wine very slowly from the bottle to the decanter and back a couple of times in order to capture the bulk of it, but it's a process worth going through if it means that you can then enjoy your wine in a glass free of grit.

Like everything else, decanters come in all shapes and sizes and vary greatly in price. In any case, as with choosing glassware, my advice would be to go for something clear, plain, free of overly fussy elements, and preferably lightweight—if you plan on pouring more than just a few glasses.

How to decant

1. How long before drinking
Old wines may not need very long to "open up," so a couple of hours (even less) will do. Young wines can happily be poured into a decanter without much attention to detail and can sit for longer.

2. Use a light
As you decant, you need to be able to spot when the sediment nears the neck of the bottle. A lit candle or medium-size upturned flashlight sitting under the bottle neck will do the trick.

3. How to hold the bottle
Hold the bottle firmly at the bottom end, so that you can see what's going on up at the neck as you pour.

4. Pour slowly
Or very slowly, if there is a lot of sediment. Pour down the side of the decanter, which can be held at an angle in your other hand. When you see the sediment reach the neck, stop.

5. Sieve
If you can't bear to lose a drop, use a filter or clean cotton cloth to catch the sediment, as long as the sediment isn't too fine and "muddy."

Temperature

Lots of people worry about going bald or getting fat. Me, I worry about the temperature of wine.

Sad, I know. Don't get me wrong, I worry about going bald and getting fat, too, but the temperature at which wine is served is a constant source of frustration for me, and I know I'm not alone. The problem is that too often we serve white wines too cold and reds not cool enough.

When you serve wine too cold, you risk masking all those lovely smells and flavors, as well as altering the wine's texture. Similarly, serve a wine too warm, and you'll notice that the alcohol becomes far more obvious and will quickly throw your wine off-balance.

While the wrong temperature might improve some poorly made wines, you can appreciate that this isn't great for either you or your wine, especially if the wine isn't cheap.

"Too often we serve white wines too cold and reds not cool enough"

Paying attention to temperature is really important—you'll find a list of recommended serving temperatures below. But, if you're stuck for time and need to alter the temperature of a wine quickly, here are a couple of tricks that may help speed up the process.

The fastest way to chill a wine is to half fill a bucket with ice and top it up with cold water. Rotate the bottle continuously in the ice for 10 minutes, at which point your wine should be cold. As this process usually results in a numb hand, nominate someone else to do it if you can. Give it a few extra minutes if you want it really cold.

Similarly, if you pull a bottle of wine from the refrigerator only to discover that it's far too cold, pour some into your glass and, cupping your hands around it, swirl the wine in the glass at the same time. The temperature from your hands will warm up the contents in the glass pretty quickly. One last thing: I'd never advocate putting wine in a microwave, a freezer, or under a hot tap. That's not to say that I haven't done it before—I just don't recommend doing it. Wine doesn't like being subjected to dramatic fluctuations in temperature.

LEFT Enjoying wine at the right temperature can be achieved no matter where you are or what you are doing. Plan ahead and drink creatively.

Serving temperatures

While there are no strict rules about temperature, this is pretty much what works for me.

1. Well chilled Nonvintage Champagne, sparkling wine, Sauvignon Blanc, Riesling, rosé, many Spanish and Italian whites, unwooded white blends, and Manzanilla and fino sherry should all be served chilled somewhere between 46°–50°F (8°-10°C).

2. Cold Vintage Champagne; fuller bodied whites, such as Chardonnay, Semillon, Viognier, Gewürztraminer, Grüner Veltliner, and Pinot Gris; reds, such as Pinot Noir, Beaujolais; and most sweet wines will all benefit from being served with a lighter chill around 52°–59°F (11°–15°C).

3. Room temperature While medium- to full-bodied reds and fortified wines should be served somewhere around 59°–63°F (15°–17°C), avoid directions that suggest serving your wine at room temperature, as this can vary enormously depending on where you live.

How to open a bottle of bubbly

While not exactly the safest method on the block, certainly the most popular way to open a bottle of bubbly appears to be that employed by our beloved racecar drivers.

This tradition dates back to the 1960s when, as a sign of his appreciation, Dan Gurney—having just won the Le Mans race and not speaking much French—did the next best thing and proceeded to empty his winning bottle of Moët onto his crew. Excluding the race held in Islamic Bahrain, it's a tradition that's held to this day.

But as fun as the "pop and spray" method may be, a bottle of sparkling wine or Champagne contains up to 6.12 atmospheres (90 lbs. per square inch) of pressure, around three times that of your average car tire. It's therefore no great surprise to discover that improperly aimed cork popping is reputedly one of the most common causes of holiday eye-related injuries.

"Hisses are cool; pops are not"

You need to be super careful when you are removing corks from pressurized bottles. Here's the best way to go about it.

Key ≫

1. Always point the bottle away from you (and others!).

2. Find and pull the rip tab. Follow the tab counterclockwise around the bottle. Remove the foil capsule.

3. Fold out the twisted wire loop, but do not untwist.

4. Place your thumb firmly over the cork, like it is a safety catch.

5. Untwist the wire loop and loosen it, without removing it. Keep your thumb firmly over the cork.

6. Close your fist tightly around the top of the bottle. With your other hand holding the base, slowly twist the bottle away from the cork rather than pulling the bottle from the cork. Remove the cork gently. Hisses are cool; pops are not.

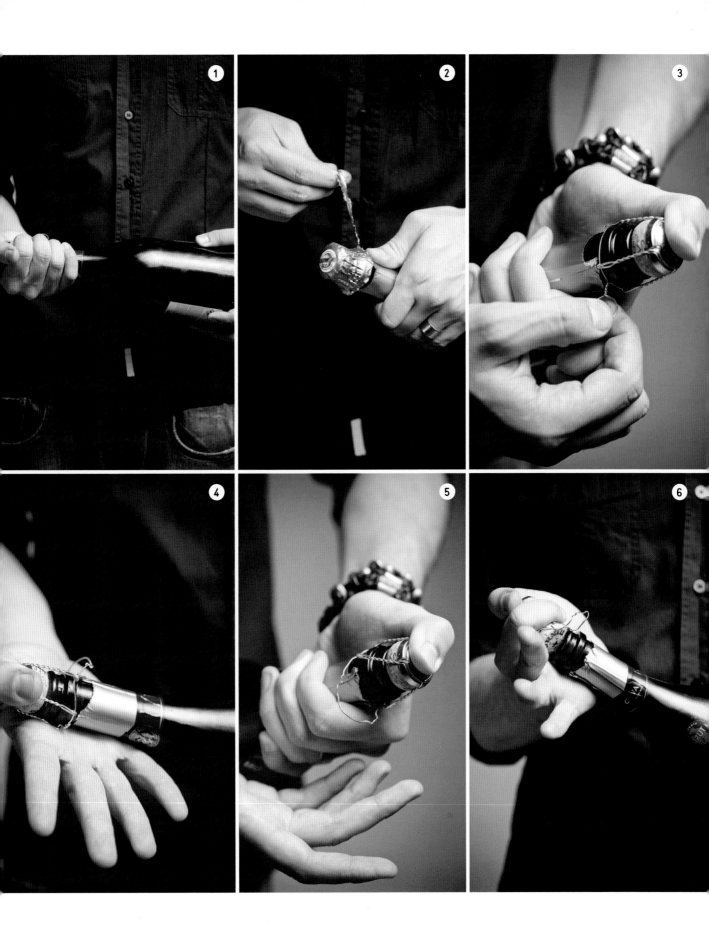

How to open a bottle of wine

I appreciate that the idea of being told how to open a bottle of wine seems almost as ridiculous as being shown how to tie your shoelaces, but you'd be surprised how many of us continue to go about it the wrong way.

Aside from making life easier, you'll also reduce the possibility of injuring yourself—and anyone who's experienced the pain of a corkscrew through the hand will no doubt agree. In any case, I doubt there'll be too much objection when it comes time to practice.

I tend to use a waiter's friend—my preferred choice of corkscrew—but any kind will do, of course, as long as you make sure the point is sharp (otherwise it will split the cork). So, I know you know how, but, just to set the record straight, this is how you should open a bottle of wine.

Key   >>

1 Holding the bottle in your non-preferred hand and your corkscrew in the other, begin by removing the top part of the foil—you don't have to take the whole capsule off, just the top quarter inch or so. This is done by making a circular cut under the lower lip of the bottle with the foil cutter on your corkscrew.

2 Placing the screw in the middle of the cork, gently twist the screw in a downward motion until the entire screw is submerged in the cork.

3 Apply the clasp to the neck of the bottle, placing your thumb over the clasp for support, then pull the lever upward and toward you. Pull gently at first until you feel the cork begin to move, increasing the pressure once you do.

4 (If you're using a "waiter's friend" style corkscrew, apply the second clasp, again supported by your thumb). Continue to pull the lever upward in one motion until the cork comes out of the bottle.

What to do if you break the cork

Relax, it's easily fixed. Depending on the condition of the cork, and how far down it's broken, there are a number of things that you can do to retrieve it.

1. Old corks

Older corks can be relatively brittle and will often all but disintegrate when you try to remove them.

If this happens, have a decanter, flashlight, and a clean cloth on standby—a candle will be fine, as will any kind of fine cotton.

Stand the flashlight upright on a flat surface, secure the cloth over the open bottle with a rubber band, and very slowly transfer the contents from the bottle into the decanter.

Aside from the cork, you may find some fine sediment that older wines often throw. You want to try to keep this in the bottle.

As with normal decanting, the torch or candle light will guide you as to when to stop pouring to avoid pouring sediment into the decanter.

2. New corks

If it's a newer cork that you've broken, you have two options.

First, you can try to operate, which is my favorite method.

This involves pulling out pretty much everything in your kitchen's utensil drawer in a bid to try to remove what remains of your cork.

The alternative option is to simply push the cork into the wine with the back end of a wooden spoon.

Once it's through, slowly transfer the contents into a decanter and serve.

Tasting wine

Learning how to taste wine is a bit like sex: not literally, but, while it's all a bit awkward at first, the more you practice, the better at it you're likely to become. Or so they say.

And as silly and awkward as all of the sniffing, swirling, slurping, and spitting may seem, it's worth persevering, as learning how to taste correctly will help you learn more about wine. If I can do it, anyone can. Begin by pouring yourself quarter of a glass.

Then follow the advice given over the next few pages. There are three basic parts to this process: using your eyes to check the wine is clean and clear; using your nose to look for fruit aromas or signs of age; and using your mouth to air the wine and explore its taste.

Once you've strung them all together, they will help you get more out of every glass you put to your lips.

You'll need to use your eyes

I appreciate that one quarter of a glass of wine doesn't constitute much in the way of fun, but having that small of an amount of wine in the glass will allow you to tilt the glass on its side and give it a good old swirl without spilling the contents—I hope.

Color jargon

• Red wine: look at the middle of the wine, then the outside rim—colors vary through inky black, purple, ruby, red, and garnet to mahogany and brown
• White wine: look for clarity and brightness—colors vary through almost clear, green, straw, and lemon to golden, amber, and tawny
• Rosé wine: look for depth of color and "pinkness" for good condition—colors vary through coral and salmon to pink

Take your glass by the stem and, with some decent overhead light and something white underneath, tilt the glass away from you at a 45-degree angle. Looking at a glass of wine can only tell you so much about it: beyond the obvious red or white, what you're seeing might give clues as to what variety the wine is, how it was produced, its age, and its condition.

What to look for

Remembering that color does not affect quality, most young wines should show bright, vibrant colors; reds will range from bright cherry to purple, while whites will go all the way from bright gold to green, to colors so pale they border on being clear. As wine gets older, red wines tend to turn slightly brown and get lighter, while white wines become darker.

Condition of the wine

Buying young wine requires a similar approach to buying fish—bright and shiny, rather than cloudy and dull. But tread with care. Some varieties are naturally lighter in color than others, and increasing numbers of wines today are being bottled unfiltered—both of which can trick you into thinking that a wine is older than it may be or, worse still, out of condition. Unfiltered wines will not be as bright or clear and tend to look darker; a white wine out of condition due to premature oxidation will darken, while a red will lighten.

Key »

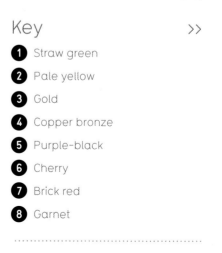

1 Straw green
2 Pale yellow
3 Gold
4 Copper bronze
5 Purple-black
6 Cherry
7 Brick red
8 Garnet

You'll need your nose

There's no sense more important than smell when it comes to tasting wine. At the top of your nose, just behind your eyes, is your olfactory nerve—the epicenter of smell and taste.

Aroma jargon

This should be a personal judgment—remember what it is you smell in a wine so that you can compare in the future. Fruit aromas speak for themselves, but the following are others to look out for:
• Tobacco
• Leather
• Spices
• Nuts
• Herbs
• Earth
• Animals
• Farmyard
• Minerals
• Smoke
• Flowers
• Eucalyptus
• Grass
• Olives
• Kerosene
• Honey
• Chocolate
• Tar
• Vanilla
• Butter
• Toast

Your olfactory nerve is the communication link between what you smell and taste and your brain. You taste berries, it tells brain. Burn your toast, and your brain will find out about it soon enough. That's why it's really important to take some time and smell what's in your glass.

Take the glass by the stem and smell. Don't swirl; just put your nose to the glass and smell. Now repeat the process, only give it a good old swirl first. To do this, find a flat surface such as a table and take hold of the stem as though you were holding a pencil. Start the liquid moving by making small clockwise rotations—almost as though you were tracing around a coin. Try to build up your speed as you go.

Aroma molecules are released from a wine's surface, so by swirling the glass you're increasing the surface area of the wine, which (fingers crossed) will give us more to smell. How far away you hold your glass from your nose is up to you; there are no set rules about this. So here

we go—give the wine in your glass a little swirl followed by a big sniff. Notice a difference?

The kinds of things that you should be looking for are fruit smells, nonfruit smells, and faults, although hopefully the faults are few and far between. While fruit smells are pretty self-explanatory, nonfruit smells are not (see box left)—some of which come through production and some of which are just characteristic of the grape variety.

Finally, if you can't smell anything, don't worry. It may be that the wine is too cold. If so, place your hands around the bowl of the glass for a couple of minutes. Or, it may just be the wine— unfortunately, some wines don't smell of much at all. In any case, give the glass another swirl and smell again. There's no limit to how many times you should smell a wine. Some you'll find you have to smell only once, while others will change in the glass, so you can o back and smell them again and again.

And, of course, you'll need your mouth

Taste is the final sense we use when tasting wine. While what we taste largely qualifies what we've smelled, the one major advantage your mouth has over your nose is that it can feel texture as well as discern sugar, acidity, and tannin.

Texture, or how a wine feels in your mouth, is really important. Wine can feel silky and fine, lean and austere, oily and round, or rough and aggressive. Beyond smell and taste, how a wine feels in your mouth will heavily influence your reaction to the overall package.

You can divide your tongue into three parts: the front senses saltiness and sweetness, the sides and middle sense acidity, and the back senses alcohol and tannin (see next page). And, almost like an echo, great wine will often resonate, going on and on long after you have swallowed it.

Take a sip—around half a mouthful is perfect. Rather than simply swallowing it, give it a good swish around your mouth. Try to suck a bit of air in at the same time—without dribbling. It's kind of like whistling in reverse. Swishing it around your mouth will give you a really good snapshot of what the wine tastes and feels like, with the air helping release more flavor.

What to look for in wine

With the wine in your mouth, think about body: is it light like water or heavy like Guinness? Think about the following:

1. Flavor
Is it sweet, sour, bitter, salty, dry, or hot?

2. Texture
Is it minerally like water from a stream or oily like, well, olive oil?

3. Balance
By balance, I mean that wine is a sum of its parts, which collectively should be seamless—kind of like looking at a jigsaw puzzle from a distance and not being able to see the individual pieces, or a band where each of the members is both playing in tune and in time with the others.

4. Length
This refers to how long you can taste the wine after you've swallowed it.

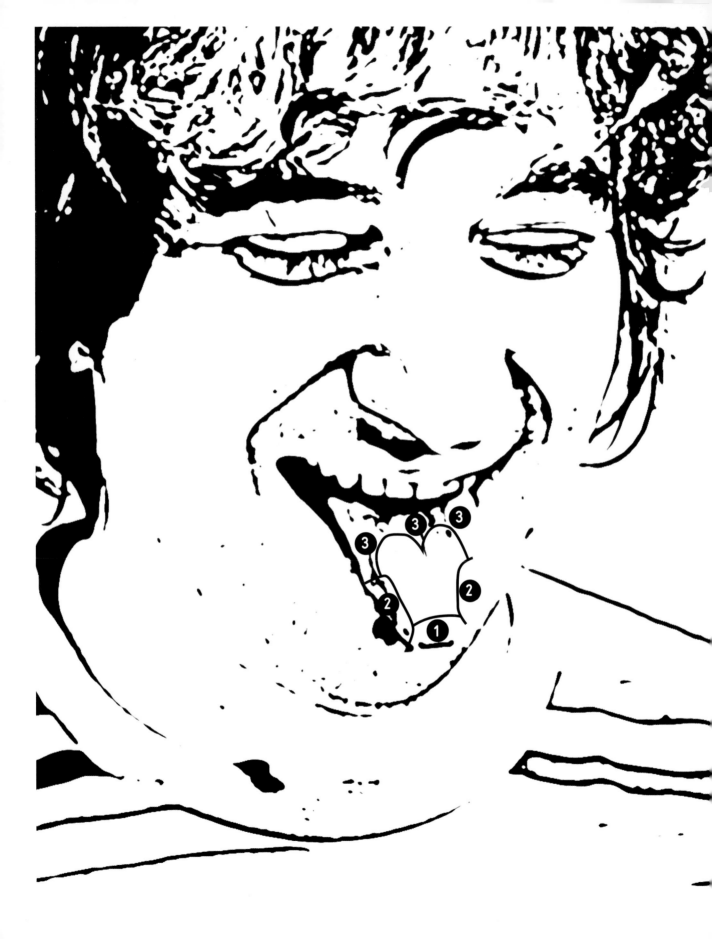

What you taste where

With something like 10,000 taste buds scattered around the roof of your mouth and tongue, your palate is the sensory equivalent of the house in the reality TV show *Big Brother*.

But here, cameras and microphones are replaced by a sea of microscopic receptors that pick up every little bit of flavor and sensation you stick in your mouth. It's therefore super important to coat the entire inside of your mouth properly by giving the wine a good swish around so that nothing will go unnoticed.

> "Acidity is registered as that pins-and-needles feeling on the sides of your tongue"

Here's a brief rundown of what's happening where . . .

Sweetness
Those of you with a sweet tooth should have no problems here. You detect sweetness on the tip of your tongue. Wines with high levels of sugar will, unless balanced by enough acidity, coat your palate and impart a cloying sensation. The best sweet wines in the world are also some of the greatest illustrations of balance between sugar and acidity.

Acidity
We're talking about types of acids that aren't harmful to us. Acidity is registered as that pins-and-needles feeling on the sides of your tongue. Some wines are more acidic than others and will make your mouth water. That level of acidity is more often noticeable right at the back of the mouth. The best German wines balance huge acidity levels with sweetness.

Tannin
Tannin is a type of acidity that comes from the pips and skins of grapes, usually red grapes. It can also come from a wine having spent extended time in oak barrels. It registers as that drying, sometimes furry characteristic that at its most extreme will coat and dry out your entire mouth. Tannin is also found in tea, especially really strong, black tea. You register tannin at the back of your palate.

Body
This is when your palate becomes like a scale and determines the weight and volume of the wine in your mouth. Wines that are higher in alcoholic strength will often feel heavier in your mouth than those that are lighter in alcohol.

Texture
Much like balance, texture is determined by a combination of sensations, including sweetness, acidity, alcohol, and tannin. It is an overall impression given by the result of each of these factors combined.

Alcohol
You feel alcohol at the back of your mouth. It comes across as a warm feeling that becomes hotter if it's not in balance with the body of the wine. A wine that has plenty of fruit flavor can support a greater percentage of alcohol compared with less fruity styles of wine.

Key «
1 Saltiness and sweetness
2 Acidity
3 Alcohol and tannin

How to spot a wine fault

Sadly, not every bottle of wine is perfect. There are two major faults you should look out for every time you open a bottle: cork taint ("corked wine") and random oxidation ("oxidized wine").

What to do when wine is faulty

• Take it back: no matter where you are—in a restaurant, at home, or away—if you purchase a bottle of wine only to find that it's faulty, please take it back. Any good restaurant or retailer will have agreements with its suppliers, who will in turn have agreements with the producers, that allow for faulty bottles to be replaced. Don't give it a second thought, even if you're borderline sure.

• Don't suffer in silence: statistics suggest that we should have more faulty bottles than we actually do, and often people prefer to suffer in silence rather than make what they think is a big deal. Please speak up!

• Don't delay: a word of warning, though, having worked in both retail and restaurants. My advice is not to return bottles that are almost empty, or six months old— that's unlikely to go down well.

RIGHT When a white wine is oxidized, it will turn a darker color, more golden. But when a red wine is oxidized, it turns lighter and more brown.

Corked wine

You can't tell if a wine is corked just by looking at it. Corked wine is not mold on the top of your cork, nor is it floating pieces of cork in your glass—you'll need to smell it. At its most obvious, a corked wine will have an unmistakable aroma of wet cardboard and mold.

Smell it once and you'll never forget it. The problem is that not every corked wine is that obvious and, even for the best tasters, it can get really difficult to tell whether a wine is corked or not. Taste it, too; cork taint will strip a wine of its fruit and leave it not just smelling flat, but tasting flat, too. Generally, the longer you leave corked wine in the glass, the more obvious these characteristics will become.

Oxidized wine

Oxidation is the effect of excessive oxygen on wine. Sometimes—due to an imperfect seal—small amounts of oxygen will seep into the wine, causing it to prematurely age, or "oxidize." The recent trend toward using lower levels of sulfur dioxide at bottling has also meant an increase in the number of oxidized wines.

Unlike corked wine, it is possible to see the effects of oxidation on wine—particularly on white wine, where at worst the liquid will turn a deep gold/copper color, while red wine will generally begin to turn brown. But the most obvious way to spot an oxidized wine is by its smell. Having lost all that lovely fruit character, you'll be left with a wine that resembles vinegar.

Other faults

There are a number of less common faults that pop up in wine. Hydrogen sulfide often shows up in wines that have been fermented in a nitrogen-limited environment and ends up smelling like rotten eggs. As a further extension of the oxidation process, acetic acid and ethyl acetate can produce smells of vinegar and nail polish remover, while bacterial spoilages such as Brettanomyces (derived from a lack of hygiene in the winery) will have your wine smelling of Band-Aids or horsehair. Nice!

How to describe what you smell and taste

Words. We use an awful lot of them in the wine world: big words, fancy words, confusing words, words that under normal circumstances—such as outside of the wine bubble—most probably mean something completely different to the rest of us.

Words such as short, flabby, funky, dirty, floral, spicy, dumb, chewy, closed, finish, hot, mature, mellow, and sexy. See what I mean? The language of wine is also its most intimidating feature. But being able to talk about wine confidently is important—especially when it comes to buying it. You don't have to know all the words, but getting your head around a couple of the most commonly used tasting terms will really help. Here are 10 to get you started.

Acidity
There are several types of acids in wine. Those you can taste will give the wine a "crisp" character and help "balance" sweetness in your wine. The acid that you smell (volatile acidity) can in some instances enhance a wine's aroma, for example Madeira and Amarone.

Balance
Balance is a collective term used to describe the relationship between the individual components of a wine. I think of wine as being a bit like a band— the aim is to have each band member playing in time, in tune, and complementing one another.

Body
This refers to the weight of a wine in your mouth. Wine is most commonly described as light, medium, or full-bodied, and this is a direct result of the alcoholic strength of a wine. More alcohol—more glycerol— means more viscosity or weight.

Bouquet
This is an old-fashioned term that refers to the aroma of a wine. Now simply described as "aroma."

Clean
This refers to a wine that has very obvious varietal character or aroma, which is most commonly a direct result of modern winemaking.

Closed
Nothing to do with having left the cork in the bottle, "closed" is a term used to describe a wine that has little smell, perhaps because of how it has been stored or transported, or simply its age. Many young wines are "closed" for a period of time after bottling.

Fruity
Often mistakenly described as "sweet," "fruit" or "fruity" is most commonly used to describe the level of both fruit smell and fruit taste in a particular wine.

Length
This refers to how "long" you can taste a wine after you've swallowed it. Similarly, a wine can also be described as "short."

Mouthfeel
As it sounds: this is how a wine "feels" in your mouth, which will usually be due to the combined effect of tannin, acidity, and flavor.

Tannic
This term is used to describe the bitter/drying taste found in red wine. As a type of acid, tannin also helps balance wine.

LEFT AND OVERLEAF The pictures shown are simply a visual aid for connecting the type of aromas and tastes you will find in wines when you are tasting. I hope you can commit some of these to memory for next time you open a bottle.

Eating

Trial and error

Food, glorious food—made even better by a well-chosen glass of wine. Food and wine matching combines a little art, a little science, and a lot of trial and error. Oh, and a touch of passion for what you are doing will take you a long way.

My approach is largely unacademic; while I understand the principles behind what I do, I'm no scientist, and I often lean heavily on instinct and luck to create decent matches. Remember, getting it wrong will ultimately help you get it right. Once upon a time, our approach to pairing food and wine was simply, red meat went with red wine, while everything else went with white. They were conservative times. The stringently observed rules weren't expected to be broken.

But times changed. We ate, drank, traveled, observed, and learned. Slowly, we became more adventurous with food and ultimately, more confident.

We wanted to know more about what we were eating, and about wine, too. It was only a matter of time before we put the two together.

In the world of food and wine matching, there are those who follow the rule book to the letter, and those who would happily watch the rule book go up in flames.

Wherever you sit, remember this: it's not so much about a wine's color as it is about the balance of flavors and textures of both the food and wine when combined.

This is the essence of good food and wine matching. Get to grips with that, and you're going straight to the head of the class.

The rules

For just about as long as we've been eating and drinking, the relationship between food and wine has split opinion. Does it go or doesn't it? Did it work or didn't it? Should you bother or shouldn't you?

When it comes to matching food and wine, there are several schools of thought. There are the traditionalists, who keep things classic and pure by creating conventional pairings. There are the nonconformists, who'd rather break the rules. Then there's the new breed: those who understand and respect the classic combinations but enjoy pushing the boundaries, too. And, of course, there are those who couldn't care less.

All of which, I should add, are fine. No matter which camp you fall into, food and wine matching is subjective and personal. I'd most likely fall in line with the new breed; I love the classic combinations, but I equally love being surprised by combinations I would never have expected to work.

I stick to the following rules: consider the weight of the food and the wine. Try to balance these two as closely and as evenly as possible, in order to create the foundation for the match.

Next, look for flavors that are similar or at least complementary to one another. Zoom in on texture and how the acidity, tannin, sweetness, and temperature of the wine will help or hinder the dish.

Making this all work is one of the hardest parts, but often it produces some of the best matches.

The following section takes you through my rules for a new way of thinking about food and wine matching.

Weight

Before flavor, weight—or the "feel" of the food or wine in your mouth—is the key to food and wine matching.

RIGHT Take a few minutes before you sit down to eat or start to plan a meal and consider the weight of the dish or the wine that will feature. Either way around, the wine has to stand up to the dish or the dish to the wine.

First and foremost, you want to try to match the weight of your food and wine evenly, so that one doesn't overpower the other.

"As the food gets heavier, so, too, should the wine"

Think of freshly shucked oysters and Champagne, a grilled piece of fish and a glass of crisp dry white, a salad of tomato and mozzarella with a glass of rosé, a juicy steak and a great big glass of red, sweet wine and blue cheese. As the food gets heavier, so, too, should the wine.

How to match weights

Balancing weight is the key. This way the subtleties and best parts of each are highlighted, rather than pushed to one side and ruined by a "heavier" partner. Now, when we talk about weight, we're not talking in "ounces" or "pounds", but rather the "feel" of either the food or the wine when it's in your mouth.

Think of how a cup of peppermint tea might feel compared to a pint of Guinness. Clearly, the beer has

a heavier and "weightier" feel to it (not to mention a more enjoyable end result).

Similarly, a steamed piece of chicken is much lighter than the same piece of meat stuck in a casserole dish and roasted with a bottle of red wine and a whole block of butter. It's really as easy as that. Get this first part right and you're halfway there!

Wine weights at a glance

LIGHT
• Riesling
• Pinot Grigio
• Gamay

MEDIUM
• Sauvignon Blanc
• Merlot
• Pinot Noir

HEAVY
• Oaked Chardonnay
• Cabernet Sauvignon
• Shiraz/Syrah

Flavor

Understanding complementary flavors will usually mean the difference between a good match and a great match.

Those of you with an above-average knowledge of food have a real head start here. Being able to identify specific flavors is one thing, but knowing which flavors will complement those you've identified is another skill altogether. This is where chefs have a real advantage. For the rest of us, here's how you might go about it.

How to match flavors
Start by looking for common flavors, or "hooks," as I call them, between your wine and food. Some of these will be more obvious than others.

> "Start by looking for common flavors, or 'hooks,' as I call them"

Let's use a good old roast chicken as an example, with its sweet, full-flavored meat that becomes richer thanks to time spent in the oven.

Assuming you've already got the "weight" thing under control, you should be looking for a wine style with a richness of flavor to match.

Next, take it a step further by thinking about complementary flavors. Chicken is terrific with lemon, thyme, garlic, butter, and mushrooms, all of which has me thinking of a full-flavored white wine, probably with a bit of oak—and more than likely Chardonnay.

Remember that it will not always be your key ingredient in a dish that might be the one to challenge a wine. Watch out for lemon and lime, chilies, and other heavyweight spices. Also, take note that some wines will challenge certain dishes —for example Gewürztraminer, Viognier, and other aromatic styles. But, see pages 108–112 and 120–129 for more of my favorite flavor matches.

LEFT AND BELOW It's worth the effort to get the flavor thing right. Think about associated flavors as well as that of the key ingredient in your dish and pick a wine that will stand up to them all.

Acidity

All wine contains naturally occurring acidity that's an essential part of every wine's makeup.

Acid helps balance a wine's flavors, adding a crisp, sometimes mouth-watering character to it. As a natural preservative, acid also plays an important role in helping wine age. You can't smell or taste acidity in wine; you simply feel it. It registers as a "pins-and-needles" sensation that you pick up on each side of your tongue.

> "Too much acidity in a dish can make your wine seem flat and dull"

How to match acidity

Beyond flavor and texture matching, other essential ingredients in the marriage between food and wine are "tools." Acid is one of these.

Often described as "sour" or "sharp," acidity is a naturally good tool for cutting, cleansing, and refreshing. Think salty battered fish washed down with a nice cold glass of bubbly—the acidity in the wine helps cut through and strip away any oily textures that are left behind, while cleaning and refreshing your palate at the same time.

In the grand scheme of things, finding a wine with the right tools is just as important as finding a wine with the right flavors and texture. Acidity in food usually comes via a squeeze of lemon or lime, or a splash of vinegar somewhere during the preparation. While a little bit is fine, too much acidity in a dish can make your wine seem flat and dull.

The same thing goes for wine—too much acidity in your wine will kill off the flavors of your meal. Finding a balance is the key.

Tannin

Tannin in wine comes from the skins and pips of grapes and is one of the best tools for matching "meaty" food.

You put the kettle on. It boils. You make yourself a cup of hot tea but, before you have time to remove the tea bag, the phone rings. You answer it, you talk, and you forget all about what you'd been doing previously.

"Tannin helps improve the color, texture, and structure of wine"

By the time you eventually return, your cup of tea is jet-black, lukewarm, and as bitter as anything you've ever put in your mouth. That right there is tannin.

Tannin helps improve the color, texture, and structure of wine. This doesn't apply to all wines, though, as tannin is far more common in reds where—different from the production of many whites—the grape skins spend more time in contact with the juice. Like acidity, tannin has no smell or taste, just texture—which, at its most obvious registers as a bitter drying character on the back of your tongue. It can feel coarse and grainy, or silky and smooth, much of which depends on the grape variety and how it was handled in the winery.

How to match tannin

Tannin is one of the true heroes of food and wine matching. Like acid, tannin is a really useful tool. Another good cutter, tannin is great at working to get through major obstacles such as protein and fat.

Italy's red superstar, Sangiovese (the main grape in Chianti), is a good example. Tough to drink on its own due to high levels of tannin, yet pair it with the right foods— meat, pasta, or anything a little bit fatty—and you'll struggle to find a better match.

Tannin levels in wine

LOW
- Most white wines
- Gamay
- Cabernet Franc

MEDIUM
- Tempranillo
- Malbec
- Grenache

HIGH
- Sangiovese
- Shiraz/Syrah
- Mourvèdre

Sweetness

Sweet food needs a wine of equally sweet proportions—get that right, and you are heading for a match made in heaven.

ABOVE Sweet wines come in many forms. The above style is Marsala, which is made in a similar way to sherry. The wine is aged in large oak casks that allow controlled oxidation and add depth and richness to the finished wine.

If, like me, you still dream about that scene in *Charlie and The Chocolate Factory*—the one where the golden ticket winners gorge themselves on grass made from minty sugar and water from chocolate—chances are you'll probably need to pay attention here, as that dream of a candy-coated food and wine utopia is harder to create than you might think.

Sweet wines are made in a different way from dry wines and can have varying levels of sugar in them. Instead of all the natural sugar being fermented to alcohol until the wine is dry, some is kept in the final wine. How much depends on the wine style being made—from off-dry to super-sweet.

How to match sweetness

Sugar poses a number of challenges for wine and, as a result, great combinations are likely to require a bit more thought.

Gelato needs Moscato, Thai food needs off-dry Riesling, pan-seared foie gras needs Sauternes, sticky toffee pudding needs Pedro Ximénez, and Stilton needs port. Well, at least that's what the rule book says. Experiment for yourselves, but know that as the weight and intensity of your food go up, so, too, should the weight and sweetness of your wine.

Tricky sweeties

Fruit comes in such a vast range, it can make it hard to match. But, demi-sec fizz and Moscato work well with most fruit, slightly chilled light red wines are excellent with summer fruit, while late-harvest Riesling, Tokay, and Muscatel all suit tropical fruit. Keep port, Madeira, Marsala, and sweet sherries for dried fruit.

Sometimes it is best to appreciate food and wine separately. Dark chocolate and rich chocolate dishes show off best alone, while the top sweet wines (Sauternes, German Trockenbeerenauslese, and Eiswein) do also.

There are a few partners for chocolate however, including southern French sweet reds (Banyuls and Maury), Amarone from Italy, and liqueur Muscatels.

Temperature

Temperature is key when it comes to both food and wine and has the ability to make or break a match.

You can tick every box. You know what you're eating, and you've found a wine with all the right flavors, the right texture, and the tools to match. And yet all that hard work can be let down by something that is completely within your control—temperature.

> "Your wine is freezing. For the next ten minutes as it comes up to temperature, it might as well be a glass of water"

You're out to dinner. You're having chicken and have settled on something full-bodied and white, Chardonnay. Your food arrives at the same time as your wine, and as it's poured, the wine makes the glass quickly frost up with condensation.

Your wine is freezing. For the next ten minutes as it comes up to temperature, it might as well be a glass of water. Meanwhile, as your wine thaws, your food is getting cold.

Understandably, if the wine has been poured, of course it's easier to warm a wine up than it is to chill it down—remember the old hands-around-the-glass trick that I mentioned earlier.

But, if you are in a restaurant, do ask for an ice bucket with water and ice for a bottle of white that is too warm—and don't wait to take an iced-up-bottle out of its bucket if it is freezing cold.

Changing seasons

The whole temperature debate can be further fueled by mentioning that tastes change depending on the temperature outside, so choose your wine according to taste.

A heavy, warming red might not be the best option for a sweltering summer barbecue, while a super-cool, racy white might not make the cut for a cozy night spent in front of the fire.

What temperature does to wine

• Weight is not so obviously affected, but to a certain degree will follow the rules for flavor

• Flavor will be less obvious if too cold or more obvious if it is warm because the aromas in wine are subdued or enhanced accordingly

• Acidity is defined better when the wine is cold—key for white wines

• Tannin becomes bitter and more aggressive in a red wine that is too cold, but softens as it warms

• Sweetness is always better chilled; the colder a sweet wine is, the less obvious the sugar and more zingy the wine

How to match food and wine

I believe that the right wine can make average food taste better, and vice versa. I also believe that food and wine matching isn't just something to wheel out on special occasions. Practice makes perfect.

Creating great matches doesn't have to be difficult or expensive—in fact, most of my favorite matches are also some of the easiest to reproduce. Take some risks—drink great Champagne with fish and chips on the beach, or enjoy a cheap red with an expensive cut of meat. You can learn from experimenting.

Take the time to befriend a sommelier, read a little (there are vast column inches dedicated to the subject), or, better still, hunt down the person who made the wine and ask them what they'd eat with it. Most of all, have fun playing around with different combinations, but never let them get in the way of simply sharing and enjoying a good meal.

Like Lennon and McCartney, some things were just meant to be. Food and wine matching is the same: some work, some don't, but half the fun is in the trying. *Bon appétit*!

By ingredient

Always consider the individual ingredients, the overall dish, and how you intend to prepare it. All of this will have a huge impact on the success of your match.

"It's fantastic with fish." How many times have you read that on a wine label? I see something like that and immediately feel my temperature start to rise. Fish how? And what kind?

I might have missed out on some crucial information, but are we now just assuming that there is only one species of fish swimming around out there, and that it all tastes the same, no matter how you cook it? Take a deep breath, Matt.

"Generally speaking, white wine is well suited to all manner of things from the sea . . . but there are plenty of great and far more exciting options to be had"

Fish, shellfish, poultry, game, meat, and cheese—each is simply a "gateway" to a more expansive and diverse range of products— each in turn with its own distinct set of aromas, flavors, and textures.

Add a whole variety of cooking methods, accompaniments, and sauces to the mix, and you begin to realize that there are an infinite number of variables to consider when you're looking for the right wine. Here are the basics to get you going . . .

Fish and shellfish

White wine goes with fish. Yes, yes, we all know that, although ordering or cooking seafood shouldn't always see you revert to the same old safe options.

Sure, generally speaking, white wine is well suited to all manner of things from the sea, but with the exception of full-throttle reds, there are plenty of great and far more exciting options to be had.

Poultry and game birds

While it all comes with a set of wings, that's about where the similarities between poultry and game birds begin and end.

At one end of the spectrum, you have chicken, turkey, goose, and pheasant—these are the milder

Good wine matches

FOR FISH AND SHELLFISH
- Cold Manzanilla sherry with whitebait or squid
- Good oloroso sherry with cooked shrimp dishes
- Light, clean, fruity whites—minus the oak—with white fish
- Full, rich whites—including oak— with mackerel, scallops, freshwater crayfish, crabs, or lobster
- Pink wines with whole roasted fish, bouillabaisse, or sardines
- Pinot Noir with salmon, trout, tuna, or sushi

FOR POULTRY AND GAME BIRDS
- Chardonnay and Viognier with milder birds, such as chicken, turkey, goose, and pheasant
- Pinot Noir and Nebbiolo with full-flavoured birds, such as duck (including mallard and teal), squab, pigeon, and grouse

LEFT Don't overelaborate on the ingredients in your dishes—keep them super-fresh and simple in the flavor department to achieve the most sublime food and wine matches.

tasting birds and are perfectly suited to full-flavored whites. Some degree of oak will really help you here. At the other end of the spectrum, you have the extreme—duck, pigeon, squab, and grouse—intense, full-flavored birds, birds that can smell so strong they have the ability to clear a room in seconds. For this reason, you need structured, earthy reds with a good balance between sweet and savory.

"Aged meat needs wines with greater intensity and richness"

Pork
For most carnivores, the bloodthirsty combination of meat and wine is just about as good as it gets. This is the territory where reds of all shapes and sizes really come into their own, although, as always, there are one or two exceptions just to keep us on our toes.

Pork is the anomaly in that it works well with both full-flavored whites and similarly heavy reds—it all depends on how you cook it: charbroiled pork chops with Chardonnay; stuffed and rolled porchetta with cavolo nero (black kale) and Sangiovese; Chinese roasted pork belly with sparkling Shiraz; sweet suckling pig with southern Italian reds, such as Primitivo, Negroamaro, and Nero d'Avola; and six-hour

slow-roasted shoulder of pork with salsa verde and Grenache. The choice is yours.

Lamb and mutton
Lamb, whether pan-fried, charbroiled, or slow-roasted—as we've already discussed—shares a mouth-watering bond with Cabernet Sauvignon, although this wine could quite easily be substituted for any full-flavored red with enough depth of flavor and dry, grippy tannin.

A few soccer seasons on and mutton, with its dense, savory edge and tougher texture, needs a wine bearing similar attributes. Look for robust, sun-soaked reds full of leathery spice and earthy flavors: Tempranillo, Touriga Nacional, and Amarone-style wines from Spain, Portugal, and Italy, respectively, will serve you well.

Veal
Moving on from old sheep to young cows, veal needs the fruit sweetness and softer structure of wine styles such as Valpolicella Classico, Carmenère, or Merlot, while its older sibling demands wines with more. Much more.

Beef
Beef calls for heavy artillery. And considerations when looking for an appropriate wine match should include how long the meat has been hung (or aged), the amount

Good wine matches

FOR PORK
- Chardonnay
- Sangiovese
- Shiraz
- Primitivo
- Grenache

FOR LAMB AND MUTTON
- Cabernet Sauvignon with lamb
- Tempranillo, Touriga Nacional, and Amarone with mutton

FOR VEAL
- Valpolicella
- Carmenère
- Merlot

My desert island dish

Almost without hesitation, my desert island dish would be *bistecca alla fiorentina* from the legendary Panzano butcher Dario Cecchini. It'd be simple: a four-finger-thick Chianina T-bone rubbed with sea salt, charbroiled over coals, and finished with good peppery new-season olive oil. That's it. No fries, no sauces, no sides, nothing. Just meat. I'd wash it down with a bottle of Sassicaia 1985, and I'd be a happy man.

Good wine matches

FOR BEEF
- Shiraz/Syrah
- Grenache
- Mourvèdre
- Carignan
- Zinfandel
- Malbec

FOR CHEESE
- Sangiovese with Parmigiano-Reggiano
- Pinot Gris with Morbier
- Sauternes with Roquefort
- Gewürztraminer with Munster
- Grenache with Berkswell
- Chardonnay with Brie
- Botrytis Riesling with Cashel Blue
- Rosé with mozzarella di bufala
- Off-dry Riesling with Comté
- Pinot Noir with Époisses
- Sauvignon Blanc with feta or chèvre
- Amontillado sherry with Lincolnshire poacher
- Manzanilla sherry with Manchego
- Prosecco with Gorgonzola dolce
- That trusty old classic, port with Stilton

of marbling (or fat) it contains, and how it has been prepared.

Aged meat needs wines with greater intensity and richness, while younger cuts need examples not only with flavor, but structure, too. If you can, be wary of heavy sauces and reductions that can really spoil the flavor of both the meat and the wine. Shiraz, Grenache, Mourvèdre, Zinfandel, Malbec, and Carignan will all be worthy contenders, although there is certainly no shortage of great steak wines out there, too.

Cheese

I love cheese for all the same reasons I love wine. Just as wine is the product of grape juice, cheese is the product of milk—every variable that can influence how a wine turns out can (and will!) also be seen in the cheese-making process.

Do I think they're good for one another? Absolutely. I get nervous just thinking about the cheese cart making its way toward my table. Cheese is not just for dinner parties, though, and you have only to travel around Europe to see that, the same as with wine, eating cheese is an everyday—almost ritualistic—part of life.

Good matches are easy to produce, largely because you are simply combining two finished products, although there are a few things that you'll need to consider along the way. Consider texture—light and delicate, soft and creamy, hard and dry, heavy and intense. Balancing the weight of both your wine and your cheese as evenly as possible is step one.

"I get nervous just thinking about the cheese cart making its way toward my table"

Next up, consider flavor—generally, the more flavor you have in your cheese, the more flavor you will need in your wine. Acidity is important, too. It's no great coincidence that high-acid cheeses, such as fresh goat cheese, work beautifully with high-acid wines, such as a young Sauvignon Blanc.

And, finally, consider mold—mold can often make dry wines seem fruitless and bitter. Both sweet and fizzy wines are good options to combat this.

RIGHT Probably the most delicious combination in the world, cheese and wine should be enjoyed together as often as possible.

By country

Ever wondered why wines that, under normal circumstances you probably wouldn't drink—and almost certainly wouldn't buy—tasted so good on vacation, but not so great back home?

Good wine for Asian and Indian food

Asian dishes can be some of the hardest to match wines to because there are no obvious partners like there are with European dishes.

• Delicate and aromatic food styles, such as Thai and Vietnamese, require wines of similar nature. Riesling, Gewürztraminer, and often those with a bit of sweetness, will be perfect.

• The richer, earthier flavors found in both Japanese and provincial Chinese cooking should have you looking at varieties such as Chardonnay and Pinot Noir.

• Heavier sauces and the use of dried fruit and spices in a lot of Indian cooking will require you to seek out wines that are richer in flavor, but softer in texture. Viognier, Merlot, and a cast of unwooded reds from warmer parts of the world should be at the top of your list.

RIGHT Food and wine matching is best explored in countries or regions that have a traditional dish and wine style.

European food

I bet you have looked back and asked why, in Italy, those big old roped bottles of house red tasted so good with nothing more than a hunk of bread and a bowl of pasta. How, in Spain, you drank glasses of ice-cold sherry before almost every meal. And, in France, how you survived on little more than cheap but enjoyable rosé by the bucketload.

While much of your enjoyment of wine is often part of a bigger emotional experience, the fact that a particular local wine works so well with a particular local dish is no great surprise, and more likely the result of many hundreds of years worth of refinement and fine-tuning.

Italian food with Italian wine, French food with French wine, Spanish food with Spanish wine, and Asian food with German wine. Yep, there are always exceptions, but, from my experience, most things go together for a reason.

Asian and Indian food

Designed to contrast a mixture of flavors and textures, Asian cooking largely concentrates on four key cornerstones: sweet, sour, salty, and hot—cornerstones that individually prove a big enough challenge for most wines, let alone having to face two or three of them at once.

"Much of your enjoyment of wine is often part of a bigger emotional experience"

Common hurdles include wines with excessive alcohol and oak—both of which have a nasty habit of overpowering delicate flavors. Overly tannic wines can be a real problem, too, especially when it comes to balancing subtle textures. Also, when combined with the raw hit of fresh chili, wines that are naturally high in acidity but low in sweetness can make spicy food seem mind-numbingly hot.

By season

I didn't always get it. In fact, it wasn't until I began working in a restaurant that I learned to understand and value the importance of seasons.

I'd never really considered how each season would have such a massive impact on the color, the smell, the flavors, the weight, and the texture of food—how each season would dictate the types of wines I could serve and the types of wines that you, as customers, would order.

I'd never considered that learning about seasonality, and the flavor combinations that each season provokes, would in turn teach me more about wine. But it has. And now I never get tired of watching it unfold.

Summer sun

Summer dishes come to life with bright and vibrant flavors. Juicy Sicilian peaches with paper-thin slices of sweet prosciutto and a drizzle of good olive oil quite literally signal the best of summer on a plate. This is the time of year for light wines—in particular, crisp unwooded whites, dry fruity rosé, and lightly chilled reds.

Earthy fall

As the summer wears into the fall, flavors became richer, earthier, and more intense. Heavy whites become light reds as those blue skies become gray.

> "As the summer wears into the fall, flavors became richer, earthier, and more intense"

The fall is the season when wild mushrooms, dried woody herbs, greens that come with the first of the season's frosts, chestnuts, rabbit, quail, pheasant, pigeon, partridge, and duck are officially ready to eat.

And it's a time of year when certain wines really come into their own—in particular, some reds and fuller whites.

LEFT AND BELOW It is not difficult to get a feel for what dish to eat and wine to drink in each season. We naturally tend to choose both by weight depending on the temperature and the number of hours of daylight.

Wines to drink

IN THE SUMMER
• Riesling
• Semillon
• Verdejo/Verdelho
• Pinot Grigio

IN THE FALL
• Viognier
• Marsanne/Roussane
• Verdicchio
• Pinot Noir
• Dolcetto
• Barbera
• Nebbiolo
• Tempranillo

IN THE WINTER
• Shiraz/Syrah
• Cabernet Sauvignon
• Zinfandel
• Malbec
• Spanish rosé

IN THE SPRING
• Chardonnay
• Sauvignon Blanc
• French rosé
• Cabernet Sauvignon
• Merlot

Winter warmers

The winter cries out for robust, hearty ingredients—slow-cooked meats, thick soups, and roasted root vegetables—dishes that can quickly make you feel warm again.

Big gutsy reds shine—wines with weight and stuffing. And then, when you've all but given up seeing the sun again, it appears, and rosé sales shoot through the roof, almost as though its consumption is a way of wooing the warmer weather.

Spring fresh

At this stage, you know that the spring is just around the corner. Chilly mornings, sunny days, the return of green to the garden, short sleeves for the overly enthusiastic—even the occasional smiling face during rush hour; like a rush of blood to the head, the first signs of spring come as a welcome relief from the bleakness of winter.

And you think the weather doesn't affect people's demeanor? Look around you. If you've been meaning to talk to someone at the bank, the spring is the time to do it.

"Like a rush of blood to the head, the first signs of spring come as a welcome relief from the bleakness of winter"

As Mother Nature's mood changes for the better, so, too, does the outlook for food lovers. This is the season for eating. Springtime brings with it an abundance of great new produce: asparagus, peas, broad beans, lamb, and great fish. And the drinking isn't so bad either, with fresh whites, delicate pinks, and soft reds the colors of the season.

Keep it simple: Sauvignon Blanc with goat cheese, broad beans, basil, lemon, and mint; rosé with the season's sweetest tomatoes you can lay your hands on; and that all-time food and wine classic, Cabernet Sauvignon with sweet spring lamb. When the spring finally arrives, a cast of fresh young wines step up to the plate and create some of the year's best food and wine combinations.

RIGHT You could pick just one food and wine combination for each season—but make sure that you challenge yourself in both departments so that you achieve the ultimate match.

Matches to try at home

This is where the fun starts. Dig out the corkscrew, roll up your sleeves, and prepare to get your hands dirty.

What follows is a handful of my all-time favorite food and wine combinations that you simply have to try, if you haven't already.

Tried, tested, and tweaked, these are the combinations that work for me. Some are popular classics, while others will no doubt cause eyebrows to be raised. But that's okay. As I say, they work for me, and that's what matters. These aren't difficult combinations to create.

They draw on ingredients that are widely available and, when combined, have the ability to take an ordinary bottle of wine, or plate of food, to another level completely.

Put simply, these are the combinations that I love. If you haven't already discovered them, I hope that you love them, too.

The best food and wine partners

Unlucky for some, these are my favorite 13 taste sensations that I recommend you try at least once.

Fino sherry and green olives

As uncool as you think they may be, fino and Manzanilla sherry are two of the greatest food-friendly wines produced anywhere in the world. The best examples are bone-dry, nutty, and with a lovely salty tang that is perfect for sparking appetites. As a result, these wines really rise to the occasion when they are paired with foods such as big, salty green olives, fresh or jarred anchovies, capers, cured meats, and nuts.

As a point of interest, both fino and Manzanilla are best drunk when fresh off the boat (ask your retailer) and should be served chilled. Buying half bottles will further maximize freshness.

Champagne and oysters

Okay, I know it's a little fancy, but it really is such a lovely combo, and the ultimate way to kick off any special occasion. I'm talking about plump, freshly shucked oysters, that taste of nothing but the sea, and a nice glass of bubbly—in this case, Champagne. With a decent match in mind, resist the temptation to add things such as scallions, red wine vinegar, pickled ginger, or fancy sorbets and instead stick to

serving your oysters with just a little squeeze of lemon or, even better, *au naturel.*

"I'm talking about plump, freshly shucked oysters, that taste of nothing but the sea, and a nice glass of bubbly"

If your budget doesn't quite make it to France, no problem; there are plenty of cheaper well-made sparkling wines from around the world that will work just as well (try examples from the U.S., Italy, Spain, Australia, New Zealand, or England).

Champagne and fish and chips

Surely not? I'm afraid so, and it happens to be one of my all-time favorites. There's something very liberating about eating fish and chips on the beach, toes in the sand, sun on its way down, decent company, and a good bottle of bubbly within arm's reach.

Wines with plenty of acidity and bubbles really come into their own here, working to cut through oil and batter, while simultaneously

RIGHT If you can get to the sun, sea, and sand, then, for me, the combination of bubbly and fish-and-chips simply cannot be beaten.

leaving your palate clean and refreshed. A little bit of salt and lemon doesn't hurt things either, although it's advisable to take it easy on the vinegar or, even better, avoid it completely. Again, it doesn't have to be French bubbly to be a perfect match, but it helps. Just don't forget the paper cups!

Sauvignon Blanc and goat cheese

The smell of spring in the air should have you automatically reaching for Sauvignon Blanc. This season's ingredients are literally made for this variety, and its pure gooseberry and blackcurrant fruit coupled with its racy acidity lay the foundation for many mouthwatering matches. And while any number of variations on broad beans, peas, mint, basil, lemon, sea salt, and really good peppery olive oil are perfectly suited to Sauvignon Blanc, it's good old goat cheese that creates the best match.

It's an incredible marriage. Two ingredients, one crisp and angular, the other pasty and chalklike, yet together they seem to disarm one another, smoothing out the hard edges as they go. Avoid goat cheese rolled in ash or, worse, pepper and generally stick to young, fresh Sauvignon Blanc.

LEFT AND RIGHT Hot, sour, and salty all make choosing a wine very tricky. Choose wines with a hint of sweetness to counteract the other flavors.

Riesling and Thai food

Day to day I eat a lot of Asian food: Vietnamese, Thai, Chinese, and Japanese. Where most European cooking proves to be pretty straightforward for wine matching, Southeast Asian and Chinese cookery definitely does not.

With palm sugar, lime juice, fish sauce, and those numbingly-hot little bird's-eye chilies (that's sweet, sour, salty, and hot all in one go) forming the basis for many Thai salads, you can probably appreciate that few wine styles are up to the job. Riesling is the exception. Look for examples with some degree of sweetness. This will help you account for most of the hurdles. Germany is home to the best of these. And as a word of warning to chili fanatics like me, be wary of how much chili you use in your cooking—even the most suitable wines have their limits.

Chardonnay and roast chicken

Chardonnay may have taken some knocks over the years, but it remains one of the most food-friendly wines around. Gone is the heavy-handed use of oak, the super-sized tropical fruit, and the "everything but the kitchen sink" approach to winemaking that put so many of you off to begin with.

The new face of Chardonnay is leaner and more focused, and as a result the wines are far better balanced and better suited to food. Which leads me straight onto an old Sunday lunch favorite.

Piping-hot oven aside—a whole chicken stuffed with lemon, butter, garlic, salt, pepper, and fresh thyme is all you need to create Chardonnay heaven. You'll need rich, sweet fruit and spicy oak to match the flavor of the bird, you'll need weight and length to carry the flavor, and you'll need focused acidity to cut through the fat and cleanse your palate. You'll need Chardonnay.

Rosé and mozzarella
As food-friendly wine styles go, rosé ranks right up there with the best of them. With the added advantage of being anything from light to heavy, sweet to dry, or somewhere in between, rosé can handle pretty much everything from a straightforward mozzarella and tomato salad all the way through to all the charred and sticky things the barbecue can manage.

That said, the freshest mozzarella you can lay your hands on, a couple of small sweet tomatoes, and a drizzle of good olive oil make one of the best, and easiest, matches for light, dry rosé you can produce. But because rosé comes in so many forms—and

rarely does it state on the label whether it's sweet or dry—it's best to ask your retailer or have a good recommendation before you buy.

Sangiovese and pizza
Friday night is pizza night in the Skinner house. If we're feeling motivated, we'll make them from scratch, covering the house in flour as we go; otherwise we'll just order them to be delivered. Whichever option we choose, the topping combinations seem to stay pretty consistent: tomato, mozzarella, capers, and anchovies; salami and fresh chili; potato and rosemary; or, the family favorite, prosciutto and rocket.

Sangiovese is the perfect pizza partner. If you're lucky enough to find yourself eating pizza in Milan, Florence, Rome, or Naples, and you're drinking from the large communal bottle of red on the table, chances are you're drinking Sangiovese. Incredibly versatile and naturally high in both tannin and acidity, Sangiovese has the structure to navigate all but the trickiest textures and still support a range of flavors, both sweet and savory. *Bellissimo*!

Pinot Noir and duck
Raw tuna, charbroiled salmon, trout, pan-roasted sea bass with lentils, mushrooms, truffles, roast chicken with morel mushrooms, coq au vin, sweet and succulent spring

RIGHT Italian food and wine matches have to be the most spectacular—Italian red wines tend to have higher levels of acidity and tannin, which makes them harder to drink alone, but when matched with a local dish, they shine.

lamb, pot-roasted rabbit with rosemary, black olives, and orange zest, quail, squab, teal, grouse, pheasant, pigeon, partridge, and all those other pretty little birds that my daughter likes to point out as we walk through the park are all perfectly suited to Pinot Noir, although none quite as well as duck. Pinot Noir and duck share an almost spiritual relationship.

At best, both are rich, decadent, and have a terrific intensity of flavor that ranges from sweet to savory. One is naturally high in fat, while the other loves nothing more than cutting through it. Together, at best, they are the ultimate combination. A word of advice, though: as Pinot Noir is a low-yielding grape variety that grows only in certain parts of the world, you'll most likely have to spend a little bit extra in order to be dazzled. I'm sure it'll be worth it.

Cabernet Sauvignon and lamb
Cabernet Sauvignon and lamb share an amazing relationship. Slow-roasted shoulder of lamb (rather than the more expensive leg) surrounded by vegetables is another favorite in our family, and the perfect Cabernet partner.

This is a tried-and-tested classic, yet, irrespective of whether you choose to pan-fry, charbroil, or roast your meat, Cabernet's core of dark fruit will naturally knit with the sweet, earthy flavor of the lamb, while the trademark dry, grainy tannin from Cabernet's thick skins will work wonders at breaking down protein and cutting through fat. To avoid overpowering your food, take a wide berth around examples with excessive alcohol and/or oak and, as always, if you're unsure, ask. Cabernet is a great international traveler, so good examples will be easy to find.

Moscato and gelato
Lemon, strawberry, pistachio, blood orange, fennel, mint—no matter what your favourite flavor of gelato may be, if you're after a foolproof dessert and wine combination, this is it. Whenever I'm lucky enough to be in Italy's northwest, this is one of the combinations I crave.

Light, sweet, and a little bit fizzy, the weight and sweetness of Moscato mirror the weight and sweetness of gelato beautifully, while the bubbles in the wine work to cleanse and refresh your palate. For the best match, stick with noncream-based gelato and sorbet, and, as all this involves is scooping gelato into a bowl and pulling the cork from a bottle, you have zero excuses for not trying it.

Pedro Ximénez and ice cream
From Jerez in Spain's south, Pedro Ximénez (PX) has an intense nose of molasses, dried raisins, spice, and spirit, while in your mouth it's syrupy, rich, and long. Serve it alongside fruitcake or sticky toffee pudding, and that's almost as good as it gets. I say "almost" because there is an easier alternative. This is an absolute no-brainer, and your guests/better half will love you for it! Grab a tub of rum and raisin ice cream (vanilla is just as good), put two scoops in a bowl, and pour PX liberally over the top as though it were hot fudge. You've made an instant classic dessert.

Liqueur Muscat and nana's plum pudding
You don't actually need a nana to make this combination work, but, as nanas seem to make the best plum puddings, it might help. Dense, moist, and rich, with spiced dried currants/citrus peel, brandy, and vanilla, there's actually very little you can do to a plum pudding to make it better. That said, a glass of Liqueur Muscat—a unique sweet wine from Australia—placed next to your bowl is a very good start.

Sporting dried raisin, rancio, spice, spirit, and wave after wave of intensity, the aromatics of great Liqueur Muscat are little short of pure magic—not to mention a match made in heaven with plum pudding, nana or not.

LEFT There are so many sweet partners. Never, never forget the end of the meal.

Sleeping

Fatal attraction

The very thing that makes wine so utterly desirable in the first place is what takes its life in the end. I'm talking about air.

As I've said before, wine is a living, breathing liquid that we consume somewhere along its journey from grape juice to vinegar. How it tastes when we drink it largely depends on what stage of the journey we drink it at.

Bottles of wine are born. Like us, they have infant years, awkward years, years of growing into their own skin, years of maturity, a peak, a plateau, and—in most cases—a slow and graceful retirement. The catalyst for change in wine is air. That said, the wine we drink today is vastly different from the wine we drank 30 years ago.

Today, we think differently, live differently, and consume differently. This is a world of convenience; a world where waiting for anything is a last resort. So why on earth would you wait years to drink a bottle of wine? I'll tell you why on pages 159–165.

Now, I want you to do something that you may not have done before. It involves buying wine to keep. Not for drinking, for keeping. Strange as it sounds, you'll get used to it. I want you to start a cellar—although on top of the refrigerator, in the closet, and next to the hot-water boiler are officially out of bounds. This is going to require some careful consideration. You'll have to think about humidity, light, temperature, and vibration—wine is sensitive to all of these things.

Your cellar doesn't need to be big or fancy, just the most appropriate spot at home to keep your wine. Oh, and along with a big padlock, a bit of self-discipline might come in handy too . . .

The opened bottle

Air has an amazing effect on wine, and the relationship between the two is as much about magic as tragedy. Anyone who has pulled the cork on a forgotten bottle only to discover how it has changed for better or worse will no doubt agree.

Air takes basic fruit smells in wine and develops them into something far more complex and interesting—something more seamless and complete than that with which you started.

But, we've all seen how quickly half an apple turns brown if you leave it out on the kitchen counter—it's the same process. Leave a bottle of wine in contact with oxygen for long enough, and eventually it'll become vinegar. This is the process of oxidation. Once it has begun, it can be slowed down, but it can't be stopped.

In this section, I will give you some tips on what to do with a bottle that has been opened.

How to keep an open bottle of wine fresh

Open bottles aren't a big problem in our house, or in the homes of most of you, I suspect—mostly because they tend to get finished.

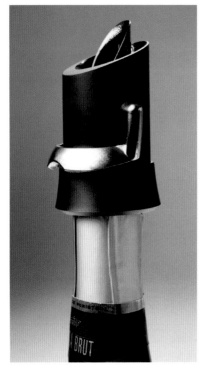

ABOVE AND RIGHT My recommendation is that if you have to leave wine in a bottle, then drink it as soon as you can, to enjoy it at its best.

But, storing leftover wine successfully can be tricky, and how long it will stay fresh will depend on what it is, where it's from, and how much liquid is left inside the bottle. Wine preservation is one area where most of us don't succeed.

"The fear of finding a half-drunk bottle covered with tinfoil, plastic wrap, or, worse still, nothing at all, is for me about as bad as it gets"

And while looking in other people's fridges isn't something I make a habit of, the fear of finding a half-drunk bottle covered with tinfoil, plastic wrap, or, worse still, nothing at all, is for me about as bad as it gets. Okay, I admit I am a little pedantic about things such as this, but if making a couple of minor changes to how you seal an opened bottle means getting an extra day or so out of your wine, then you should get pedantic about it, too.

It is also worth noting that, generally, young wines will better stand up to air once opened than older wines will; if you are opening a fine old wine, then use this very excuse to finish the bottle.

Wine accessories

An ever-expanding wine accessories market means that there are a million and one different options available to you, and, for what it's worth, I've tried most of them: rubber seals, vacuum pumps, nitrogen, even Mom's foil-and-rubber-band method. And do you know what? Most, not all, but most do pretty much the same thing as simply shoving a cork back in the bottle. I kid you not.

So, should you find yourself wondering what to do with half a bottle of wine—besides drinking it—here are some ideas.

Spring-loaded stoppers (left)

These are most commonly used in the preservation of Champagne and other sparkling wines. They don't remove trapped air, instead they create pressure in order to retain bubbles. They're a pretty simple yet effective device and a much better alternative than a spoon! You can get these type of

stoppers for still wine, but in this case, they do pretty much the same job as reapplying the cork.

Vacuum pumps
These work by removing as much of the excess oxygen from an opened bottle of wine as possible prior to creating an airtight seal. They're great for infrequent use. A rubber stopper is placed into the open bottle, and a hand pump sucks out the remaining air. But, while these pumps are good at removing trapped air, they can also remove much of the wine's aroma.

Nitrogen
As extreme as it sounds, spraying compressed nitrogen into an open bottle of wine should help preserve its contents. The nitrogen spray will displace any remaining oxygen before settling to form an airtight blanket over the wine, protecting it from air. Requiring no movement or pumping, this method is also one of the gentlest forms of wine preservation. The reality all depends on how high-tech your equipment is.

Refrigeration (above)
Refrigerating leftover wine will dramatically help preserve its life span, whether the wine is white, red, sweet, or fizzy. By chilling leftover wine, you're effectively slowing the chemical reactions that cause wine to oxidize.

Wherever possible, try to reduce the amount of oxygen in the bottle prior to putting it in the refrigerator. This can be done by decanting into a smaller bottle.

Decanting
Yes, simply decanting what's left of your wine into a smaller bottle will help keep it fresh for longer. How much longer will all depend on what it is, but by reducing the oxygen-to-wine ratio, you will significantly slow the process of oxidation. Soft drink bottles are often good here. Make sure that they have been properly rinsed with hot water (no detergent!) and that they have an airtight stopper.

The unopened bottle

Wine is a complex mix of hundreds of molecules that form as the grapes grow, the juice ferments, and the wine ages. What's more, wine needs oxygen to evolve and age. This is a slow and gradual process that occurs over a long period.

Air influences wine in two ways, the first of which occurs in the bottle. Contained within a wine's makeup are millions of microscopic oxygen molecules— more than enough to ensure that they'll have an effect on the liquid in which they're suspended. Without help, this is destined to be a mighty slow process.

Secondly, wines bottled under traditional cork—a naturally permeable material—allow for a slow and steady transfer of oxygen between the liquid contained within the bottle and the outside world. This process has a much more rapid and noticeable effect on the contents within.

But it's really important to remember that not all wines age at the same rate, nor will you always end up with the same result. These things will be determined by what your wine is, where it's from, and how it was made.

Will all wine get better with age?

If only that were the case! While plenty of wines do improve with time, plenty don't. Bad wine will not get better with age—it just becomes old bad wine.

You have to start with a great raw product. There are both certainties and uncertainties that determine how a wine will develop. What we know for sure is that not all grape varieties and styles are built to last, and there's no guarantee that those that will endure will improve. The uncertainties surround production and storage. It's a little bit like cooking. You can start out with the best ingredients in the world and still manage to mess up the recipe. Careless production will often affect a wine's ability to age, as will keeping the finished product under the wrong conditions. Although it's still largely a mystery why wine develops with age, what we do know is that these changes occur due to continuous chemical exchanges within a wine's molecular structure (see below). As a result, there are several noticeable changes that occur, which I describe on the next page. Most importantly, it's worth remembering that it's always better to drink a wine too young than too old.

RIGHT The dusty old bottle is sure to conjure up romantic thoughts, but beware, because not all wines are built to last.

How wine structure changes during aging

1. Polyphenols in red wine
These are color compounds in the grape skin that transform into:

- Tannin
  Tannin molecules combine together over time to precipitate out into the wine as sediment—these are light in color, with orange hues.

- Anthocyanins
  Dark and purple in color, these molecules do the same as tannin, but more quickly, which leaves the lighter tannin and color in the wine.

2. Controlled oxidative effects in white wine
Through oak aging, wood allows a certain amount of oxygen to enter the wine, which darkens it slightly and makes it more golden.

3. Caramelization in white wine
In sweet wines, the sugar that has been left unfermented in the wine will caramelize over time, giving a darker wine with a deeper golden color.

How wine changes over time

Add air to the equation, and things really start to get interesting. Slowly, oxygen will react and feed on the wine's molecular makeup, altering color, aromas, flavors, and texture as it goes. It's as natural, yet as complicated, as that.

Color

The appearance of a wine is often one of the first things you notice. As a rule, white wines tend to get darker with age, while red wines will often get lighter.

Consistency of color is also a good indicator of age. Tilting your glass away from you, you might notice that older wine will often fade and change color toward the edge of the rim. Many red wines will begin to turn brown over time.

Aromas

The smell of old wine can be incredible; so good that it almost seems a shame to drink it. But the smell of some older wines can also come as a shock—especially if, like most of us, you're used to drinking younger wines. To start with, primary fruit aromas—all the lovely fresh fruit smells that we look for in young wine—will slowly develop and disappear. Bright fruit aromas make way for darker, richer ones, then you begin to notice what we call "secondary aromas." These are nonfruit aromas that develop with the wine and range from spice, nuttiness, and earth all the way to tobacco, farmyard, mushrooms, and leather.

Flavors

Just like aroma, the flavors found in your wine will mature with time. Fresh and fruity becomes darker and richer. It is also worth mentioning here that, if you are drinking a young wine and an old wine together in one sitting during a meal, the younger wine will taste fuller but less complex than the older wine. The best way to solve the order-to-drink question is to match the wines to the food you are eating.

Texture

As wine gets older, the way it feels in your mouth compared with how it felt when it was young changes considerably. Most obviously, it becomes "thinner" in body. This happens because compounds that have always been suspended in the wine (things such as tannin and color) begin to solidify and "drop out" of the wine, forming what we refer to as "sediment."

Acidity, which can feel "sharp" or "fizzy" in young wine, will often soften up to the point where it is no longer noticeable. In red wine, tannins that are present as complex chains of polyphenols will join other chains to form a much longer and more complex chain, giving the impression of a softer mouthfeel.

LEFT Paying attention to the nose of a wine gives you a broader view of that wine than if you simply drank it without taking notice of the aromas. As a wine ages, it develops an array of unusual aromas—take the time to savor them all.

Wines to drink young

These are the varieties and styles that you should be drinking as soon as they hit the shelves. They're like the sprinters of the wine world.

At a glance—wines to drink young

- Prosecco, cava, and many cheaper New World sparkling wines
- Aromatic whites: Semillon/ Sauvignon blends, Sauvignon Blanc, Gewürztraminer, Verdelho, Verdejo
- Most Pinot Grigio
- Most rosé wines
- A handful of reds: Beaujolais, Dolcetto, Barbera, New World Merlot
- Most fortified wines and sherry

In some cases, they're wines that rely on their youth for freshness, while in others, it's techniques employed during production that prevent them from further improving with age.

Sparkling wines

Prosecco, cava, and many cheaper examples of New World sparkling wines are ideally suited to drinking young—preferably within the first 12 months of release —in order to preserve the clean aromas, flavors, and vibrant acidity.

White wines

For pretty much the same reason, highly aromatic styles, such as Sauvignon Blanc—New and Old World examples—Semillon/ Sauvignon blends, Gewürztraminer, Verdelho, and Verdejo are never better than when they first hit the shelves. Most Pinot Grigio also falls into this category. These are immediate wines, many of which begin to dull and lose all those lovely aromatics after 12–18 months in the bottle.

Rosé wines

Rosé fans should take notice here, as most pink wines rely on aromatic freshness for appeal, so should be treated in the same way as the aromatic whites listed above.

Red wines

A handful of red grape varieties and styles, including those that don't spend time in oak, are also generally suited to early consumption; Beaujolais (Gamay), Dolcetto, Barbera, and Merlot are all good examples of red wines that can be drunk young and also slightly cooler if preferred—which works well with some spicy food.

Fortified wines and sherry

And, finally, production methods will prohibit the development of both fortified wines and sherry— the additional spirit working to preserve aroma and flavor. And although these do keep, it is better to enjoy them sooner than later, as the fruit vibrancy fades if fortified wines and sherry are kept too long—especially with deliciously dry and fresh sherries, such as Manzanilla or fino.

RIGHT The beauty of most wine is that it's made to drink immediately, to make way for the next vintage coming through.

Wines to hang onto for a couple of years

Just a couple of years in the cellar will help many wines improve—and mean less waiting for you.

At a glance—wines to hang onto for a couple of years

- Nonvintage Champagne
- New World Chardonnay, Marsanne, and Viognier (and Marsanne/Viognier blends)
- Pinot Noir, Syrah and Shiraz, Nebbiolo, Tempranillo, and Grenache

RIGHT You can even try keeping cheaper wines that might not be expected to age for a couple of years. The result can be a very welcome surprise.

Besides helping soften aggressive acidity in young wines, cellaring some wines for a year or two can also make a difference to harsh tannins that are often found in young reds, which need time to round and integrate. Here's an idea of which varieties and styles will benefit most from a short stint somewhere cool, dark, and quiet.

Champagne

There's a common misconception that nonvintage Champagne will not improve with time: in fact, it will. Producers aside, most Champagne houses and top-end sparkling wine producers make a number of different wines. Nonvintage Champagne/sparkling wine is the most common and sets the tone for a house style. It's a jigsaw puzzle of a wine assembled from multiple years and is intended to remain consistent year in year out. Many nonvintage styles will soften and become more golden in color, while taking on honeyed and rich citrus smells and flavors with age.

White wines

With aging potential and compatibility with food now the focus of much New World Chardonnay, this is a style that will definitely benefit from a few years unwinding in the cellar. A couple of years ago this may have been an altogether different story. Marsanne and Viognier (or blends of the two) can also show themselves well after a few years in the bottle.

Red wines

The main benefit here is for red varieties such as Pinot Noir (especially from the New World), Syrah and warm-climate Shiraz, Nebbiolo, Sangiovese, Tempranillo, Grenache—these will all often benefit from a few years in the cellar, allowing them to soften and "knit" together.

Tracking a wine's development

If you are experimenting with aging wines for a couple of years, why not buy six bottles of the same wine. You can then chart the wine's development by opening individual bottles at specific time intervals, such as when you buy it, six months later, then a year later, and so on. And, if you find a wine that is developing more quickly than you thought it would, you can drink the other bottles at the optimum time.

Wines to hide under the house

And then there are those few varieties and styles that are best if left alone —not forever, but for long enough to allow them to unwind, soften, round, develop, and mature.

At a glance—wines to hide under the house

• Vintage Champagne and sparkling wine
• Riesling, Semillon, and Old World Chardonnay (including Chablis)
• Cabernet Sauvignon
• Botrytis-affected sweet wines and vintage port

RIGHT If you are going to invest in great wine, make sure you invest in the right kind of home for it. Correct cellaring is key to keeping the wine in its best condition and ensuring its best value.

These are the sleepers: the varieties and styles built to go the distance—the wines with real staying power.

Champagne
Vintage Champagne/sparkling wine is produced only in particular years when the producer believes Mother Nature has been truly kind to them; its aim being to provide a crystal-clear snapshot of that year. The best examples age superbly due to searing levels of acidity and great balance.

White wines
Similarly, while often delicious and mouthwatering in their youth, both Riesling and Semillon have an uncanny ability to go on and on, comfortably outliving most other varieties—white or red. The greatest examples of both can live for decades, evolving into rich, toasty, citrus-laden wines with incredible depth and purity. Old World Chardonnay, including Chablis, often needs time to unwind and evolve, with primary fruit flavors making way for some lovely secondary aromas and flavors.

Red wines
Of all the red grape family, Cabernet is the survivor. Thick skins mean more tannin that, provided you have the fruit to match, can make for some extraordinarily powerful and long-lived wines.

Sweet wines
Finally, both botrytis-affected sweet wines and vintage port will often need decades in the cellar before they begin to show their best. The only downside is that you'll need the patience and self-discipline to match!

Choosing wine to age long-term
Investing in wine can involve significant amounts of money, and so the choices you make are critical. I will cover this in more detail later, but use all the reference there is available—from the Internet, through specialist wine merchants and brokers, to magazines and books (from around the world).

The cellar

Shortly after getting my first job in the wine industry, one of my best friends turned 21. I thought a bottle of something really special—one that he could save for decades to come —would be a fitting way to mark the occasion.

Penfolds Grange 1991 was just out, and so, taking into consideration my staff discount, together with how little I knew about the value of what I was buying, I settled on a bottle of Australia's most iconic wine as the perfect gift for a 21-year-old whose hobbies ranged from sex to drugs and rock and roll. He seemed genuinely touched by the gesture too, but his dad—a big wine-lover—was horrified, and with good reason. You see, the problem was that Matt lived in the kind of student commune that made *Animal House* look like *The Brady Bunch*.

For years, that bottle of Grange lived at the back of his closet, escaping the clutches of many 4:00 A.M. drinking sessions until one morning when—much to Matt's horror—he returned home just in time to find one of his roommates levering the cork from his precious bottle.

This is just one of the many reasons why you need a cellar.

A story about storage

If you have a few special bottles of wine lying around somewhere they shouldn't be, you need to move them. Remember, wine is alive, and you should be taking care of your bottles well.

In 1916, the schooner *Jönköping* left the Swedish port of Gävle, bound for Finland. On board were 4,400 bottles of 1907 Heidsieck Champagne "Goût Americain." intended for the officer corps of czarist Russia. Almost at her destination, the *Jönköping* was stopped off the Finnish coast by the German submarine *U22* and sunk by a dynamite charge, killing all on board and sending her wreck, complete with precious cargo, to the seabed below.

Almost 80 years later, with the aid of sonar recovery equipment, two divers located the *Jönköping*, and so the salvage operation began. The two divers couldn't believe what they had found; there among the wreckage lay much of the Champagne.

Miraculously, both the bottles and corks had withstood the pressure, and the dark, ice-cold water had provided a near state of suspended animation, serving to protect and preserve the bottles' contents. The two divers quickly acquired the rights to the cargo, carrying an estimated value of between US$20 and 70 million, and the recovery continued.

The salvaged Champagne went on to fetch record prices at Christie's auction house, with one European buyer paying in excess of US$4,000 per bottle—to this day the highest auction price ever paid for a single bottle of Champagne.

What we can learn from this story? Finding somewhere with the right conditions to keep your wine is essential. While the idea of keeping wine might sound very sophisticated, the reality is that it's not difficult to create simple and affordable storage, and you don't need to know much about wine.

LEFT It's unlikely that you are ever going to go after a wine such as this, but attending a wine auction can be an intriguing way of learning about a wine's history.

The location of your cellar

I can understand how the idea of having a wine cellar might put you off. For most of us, the idea of starting a cellar is about as much of a priority as starting next year's tax return.

At a glance—wine cellar essentials

- Temperature: 51.8°–59°F (11°–15°C) and stable
- Humidity: 50–70 percent
- Light: ideally completely dark
- Vibration: none

RIGHT A "drill-down" cellar is a bit of a luxury, but, if you're in a position to install one of these, it can add value to your property.

After all, aren't cellars just for the rich, really hardcore wine enthusiasts? Aren't they the sacred domain of those who persist in wearing bow ties despite the fact that they went out of fashion at least two decades ago? No.

Basic or sophisticated
You don't need to know much about wine to have a cellar. And your cellar can be as basic as a simple stack of cardboard boxes in the corner of a room or as sophisticated as a state-of-the-art, pimped-out cavernous underground space.

Basically, if you have more than a few bottles lying around, you should store them correctly, and you're probably better off with a designated space in which to do this. It doesn't matter how glamorous your space is, just as long as it meets a few fundamental requirements along the way.

Features a wine cellar needs
There are some things you need to consider before you get busy cleaning out the hallway cupboard in preparation for your new wine collection. Wine is a highly sensitive liquid that's not all that fond of change. It doesn't like dramatic fluctuations in temperature, although humidity is really important. It's also sensitive to light, and not a big fan of vibration.

"After air, the most common killer of wine is temperature"

Now, as high maintenance as your new hobby might sound, these factors are all really important, as incorrect storage will shave years off the life of your wine.

Temperature
After air, the most common killer of wine is temperature. Stability, without fluctuation, is what you need—a nice cool spot that remains relatively consistent in temperature. While gradual rises in temperature over a period of time are nothing to be too alarmed about, sharp and dramatic rises are.

In a perfect world, you're looking for a stable temperature somewhere

between 51.8°–59°F (11°-15°C). A digital thermometer will be the best way to help you determine this.

I can't stress how important this is—get it wrong, and you risk spoiling your wine. Simple as that. Too hot, and you risk leaking bottles and expanding corks. Too cold (while not as bad as too warm), and you risk your wines forming deposits; these can be crystal-like formations in white wine (often mistaken for glass) and heavy sediment in reds.

For what it's worth, red wine—especially the robust, full-bodied kind—tends to be the most resilient to temperature change, while delicate whites, obviously, are the most susceptible to damage.

Humidity
The level of humidity in your cellar is also crucial; you must have some moisture in the air. Ideally, this should be upwards of 50 percent, but not above 70 percent. The reason for this is primarily to keep the corks moist—this is also why we keep most bottles stored lying down. If corks are allowed

to dry out, they will lose their natural elasticity, begin to shrink, and become brittle. As you can possibly imagine, this can cause all sorts of problems in regards to oxidation. Basic humidification units are available from most good hardware stores.

Light
It's no great coincidence that most wine is bottled in green glass. Wine is light-sensitive, and prolonged exposure—especially to direct sunlight—will irreversibly damage your wine. The perfect cellar should be dark, and any lighting that you wish to install should be soft, low-wattage fixtures instead of harsh direct light, such as halogen or fluorescent lighting.

Vibration
Wine really doesn't like being moved around. Remember that wine develops due to continuous chemical exchanges that occur slowly over time. Movement can upset this process, and you need to be especially careful when it comes to vibration. Sound is often the main offender here, as are the vibrations due to your

cellared wine's proximity to roads and windows.

Location
I'm afraid that on top of the refrigerator, next to the boiler, or in the back of your closet is no longer going to cut it. Your wine deserves better.

With each of the above factors taken into consideration, you should be making a shortlist of suitable places. And if you can't find one, create one. This might require you to think outside the box. But, wherever you choose, take into account all the points mentioned above.

Standing up or lying down?
Traditionally, we've more often done it lying down—cellaring, that is. We lay bottles on their side not only to keep the corks moist, but also because it is a simple, organized, and space-effective method of storage. But the rise of the screw cap has brought about an alternative: the era of the stand-up cellar. Obviously, with no cork to keep moist, it's fine to keep your bottles upright.

Cellaring options

There are all kinds of options available—from simple self-assembly wine racks that can be put together by even the most DIY-challenged individuals, through to large storage facilities that will manage and cellar your entire collection.

What you need depends on your wine collection. Here is a range of cellaring solutions, along with brief descriptions as to how they differ from one another.

Short-term options

These are the basic and most affordable self-assembly wine racks that you can get from most good homeware stores. Most will hold one or two dozen bottles lying horizontally and are suited to short-term storage. But, if you have any bottles that you're especially fond of, I urge you to refer to the previous pages regarding correct storage conditions.

Refrigeration

The increased popularity of wine has bought about a huge need for effective storage. And, as many of us don't live in spacious stately homes, the need for compact design has never been greater.

A number of companies specialize in wine refrigeration units. These can range from the size of a small bar fridge all the way through to made-to-measure deluxe units. The advantage of this type of unit is that it can regulate temperature and humidity within a number of different zones. This means that you can effectively keep red, white, and sparkling in the same unit, but at three different temperatures. They are effective, but obviously the most expensive.

Drill-downs

While not terribly practical if you happen to live in a top-floor apartment, the drill-down cellar is great for ground-floor apartments or houses that are short on space.

As the name suggests, a large hole of varying size is drilled into the floor of the property. A set of spiral stairs is then fitted, and wine racking is attached to line the inside wall; access is usually by a trapdoor in your floor. Installing this type of cellar can add real value to your property.

Professional cellarage

If you have the collection but lack the room, or the inclination to manage it, why not get someone else to do it for you?

Nowadays, there is no shortage of professional cellars. For a fee (often by the case), these businesses will collect your wine, catalog it, store it in perfect conditions, advise you—should you wish—on when best to drink it, help you to sell it at an auction, and deliver your bottles back to you when you need them.

If you can bear to be without your wine—some of us can't—and you can afford it, professional cellars are great places to keep your wine.

Doing it cheaply

Relax. If you're worried that you're risking your wine because you don't have the funds or space for a cellar, it's okay, there is a way. Provided that you can find somewhere with a stable temperature and away from light and vibration, worst-case scenario, both flat-packing cardboard and styrofoam wine boxes will be fine.

While I don't recommend that you keep your wine this way for a long period of time, this method will prevent light damage and maintain a reasonably stable temperature, as well as providing limited protection for your bottles.

The investment

Partying, food, transportation, rent or mortgage, and bills (roughly in that order): there are a million and one ways to spend your hard-earned cash. The reality for most of us is that investing in wine—wine that we're not intending to drink for some time—isn't especially high up the list, if it's on the list at all. For most of us, the idea of investing money in wine is odd.

Once you've decided to invest, however, the first thing you need to do is figure out why you're investing. What do you plan to do with the wine? Are you going to sell it or drink it? It's important to be clear on this point, as your decision will largely determine what you buy going forward.

In this section, I will take you through the dos and don'ts of investing and the factors that influence the value of your wine —which I hope will help you make the right decision.

And, finally, you don't need tons of cash to fund your investment. Do it slowly and surely— even if it's just one or two bottles a month.

Why should you invest in wine?

If you plan to invest in wine for financial gain, provided you spend your money wisely, the returns can be significant.

What are the risks?

Obviously, you are in possession of a perishable product and therefore —especially if it is purchased as an investment—you will need to ensure that it is cared for correctly.

• Wine prices can go down as quickly as they can go up. If the market takes a downturn, chances are that some of your wine's value will be shaved from it.

• The cost of selling your wine can be expensive. Brokerage fees can be huge if you need to sell it quickly.

• Counterfeit wine is everywhere. You need to make sure that not only are you dealing with a reputable source but that you are also confident in your merchant's abilities. Ensure that you are dealing with a reputable merchant, as many go broke and fleece their customers in the process—you may even end up losing your wine.

For this reason, many choose to put their money into wine rather than into more conventional investments, such as shares. Unless you know what you are doing, you will need the help of a merchant or broker who can design a portfolio of wine for you based on your budget, buy the wine for you, store it, monitor and calculate its growth, advise you on when to sell, and help you sell it. For all of this, they'll take a cut. How much will depend on how quickly you need to get rid of your wine and on how much you have to sell.

Invest for love

As well as investing for money, you might invest for love. I have never bought a bottle of wine to sell. I'm not suggesting that you do the same, and I have no problem with those who sell their wine, but I just love the fact that wine changes with time and becomes more interesting. And I love the fact that each bottle represents a snapshot of a time and place—like a liquid time capsule. It's an amazing thing to purchase a wine you like and put it away to age. It's incredibly rewarding when you finally drink it.

How much money will you need?

How much you will need to invest will all depend on why you are investing. If it's for personal benefit, set yourself a budget and stick to it. Of course, you can be flexible if you are having a tight month financially.

> "I love the fact that each bottle represents a snapshot of a time and place—like a liquid time capsule"

If you are investing for financial gain, your investment is likely to be considerably greater. What you buy will be focused on consistent and proven performers, all of which —because of established and well-earned reputations and growing international demand—will be likely to set you back a little financially.

What determines the value of wine?

Does all wine go up in value? The (very) short answer to this question is no. As I've already said, bad wine does not get better with age.

Even with great wine, there's no guarantee that it's going to go up in value. There are many variables that will help inflate the price of a wine: region, vintage, production, volume, and, most importantly, the reputation of the producer. These will all play a role in determining what a wine will end up costing.

Factors influencing the value of wine

1. Region
Think of wine regions like suburbs. Some are fancier than others and, as a result, property in those areas is often worth more. But what makes a wine region fancy? In the case of Burgundy in France, it's a complex equation of soil, climate, miniscule productions, producer integrity, and, most importantly, a proven track record for producing excellent wine. These factors will all influence the price of wine from a particular region.

2. Vintage
One of the best things about the world of wine is that no two vintages are ever the same. Mother Nature has a way of putting her stamp on each and every year—with some turning out better than others. In great years—years where absolutely everything goes right in the vineyards for the producer—you may see a general increase in prices. Similarly, if yields are down and there's less volume than normal, prices may also rise. But rarely do we see a reduction in prices!

3. Producer
Great producers will make great wines, even in the toughest years, and therefore have established and well-earned reputations. The problem is that these people rarely make enough wine to go around and, as a result, demand will outstrip supply, further forcing up the price of the wine. As the wine gets older, its availability will be greatly reduced—probably as most of it will have been drunk—and suddenly your wine becomes even more precious because of this.

The "dos" of buying wine

Investing in wine can be incredibly rewarding, but it can also be a risky business. As with buying any second hand goods, you do need to be careful.

Here are the key things to ensure that you do—and on the next page you'll find the key things to ensure that you don't do.

Do find yourself a decent merchant or broker

Regardless of how much you know about wine, a decent merchant or broker is invaluable. This is your key to good investment. Do some research to make sure that you are dealing with a well-established and reputable investor.

Do shop around

Aside from giving you a better understanding of the market rate, shopping around will often unearth the same wines for different prices. But no matter what, make sure that you're buying from a reputable source—especially if you are planning to spend a significant amount.

Do pay attention to the critics

Love them or hate them, they are incredibly influential, and their opinions will often affect the final price of a wine. Find out which critics are regarded as the ones to follow, subscribe to their newsletters and Web sites, and try to get onto their recommendations early!

Do insure your wine to its full market value

This covers you in case the merchant you are dealing with is declared bankrupt. It will also cover you in case anything unforeseen happens to your wine while it is being stored. Keep an eye on auction results to help monitor the value of your wine.

Do buy in bulk

If you can manage it, buying in lots of three or more dozen at a time can help maximize your return—especially since restaurants and other trade buyers will be looking for volume.

Do, where possible, check the provenance and condition of the wine

Counterfeits aside, it's really important that you know where and how any wines that you're thinking of purchasing have been stored. Check that fill levels are acceptable, check labels for light damage, and inspect capsules for leakage.

RIGHT It is essential to make sure that the bottles you invest in come from where and who they say they do. Counterfeit bottles are in circulation, and so going through a reputable merchant or broker is the most secure way of investing.

The "don'ts" of buying wine

There are pitfalls to buying wine for investment, and you need to be aware of them to stop you from running into trouble.

Don't bank on a quick return

Making real money from wine takes time. Some wines will appreciate far more quickly than others, but as a rule you'll probably have to wait. The reduced number of bottles left in circulation, coupled with a wine entering its drinking window, will force prices to rise.

Don't just buy any old wine

If you're buying wine for financial purposes, it's really important to separate your personal taste from wines that will actually make you money. This will make you a far more successful investor than those who fall into the trap of buying favorites, thinking that they'll earn them huge returns, when there are no guarantees.

Don't buy loose bottles

The value of a wine is greatly reduced if prospective buyers cannot be convinced that the wine has been cellared correctly—as a result, wines that you intend to sell should remain sealed in their boxes. Aside from keeping your investment safe, unbroken cases will always fetch the highest prices.

Don't believe the hype

Make sure that you do plenty of research on whatever it is you intend to buy. It's really easy to get overexcited about wine investment—especially since the media usually report only the extreme cases. These reports are rarely representative of the market.

> "It's really easy to get overexcited about wine investment—especially since the media usually report only the extreme cases"

Don't keep your wine in your garage

After all that we've talked about, please make sure that you keep your investment somewhere safe. Most merchants will be able to advise you on where you can keep your wine and, for a fee, many will happily keep it for you.

LEFT Resist the urge to buy single bottles as an investment—you have no guarantee that they have been taken care of correctly. And forget personal taste; be objective about your wine choice.

Well-being

A few things I've learned about wine and well-being

There was a time not so long ago when wine was seen as the medical world's great hope. The combination of alcohol and acidity proved to be a winning combination in tackling all kinds of injuries and illnesses, and its healing properties were praised and prescribed by doctors all around the globe.

However, in the latter part of the twentieth century came advances in medicine and technology, not to mention different ways of thinking. For the first time, the healing properties of wine were scrutinized to scientific standards.

Today, with modern thinking, further medical advances and interest in subjects such as the French Paradox (the term given for the fact that the French have lower rates of heart disease and cancer, together with a greater life expectancy, despite their higher rates of smoking and their enjoyment of a diet relatively high in fat), many experts would now argue that most healthy people who drink wine regularly and in moderation remain healthy.

But, it is important to recognize that these benefits should not be viewed without caution.

* If you are worried or need more advice on how drinking wine will affect your health, make sure you that talk to your doctor about it as soon as possible.

There are very few days in my life when I do not drink wine. It's my job, and, besides, I enjoy a couple of glasses of wine with my dinner. Although, in saying that, rarely do I drink more than that during the week, and I virtually never get drunk on wine. I'm conscious of what I drink because I work in an industry where alcohol dependency is common. The wine industry is an easy place to hide alcohol problems, and I've worked alongside a number of people with serious alcohol dependencies and watched a couple of close friends become alcoholics in the process. It's the worst kind of occupational hazard I can imagine.

I am not a doctor, and I am not here to tell you how much you should or shouldn't be drinking. I simply want to help if you're worried so that you can do some further research or seek professional help. At the end of the day, only you know what's best for you. For more information on alcohol dependence or alcoholism, I suggest that you visit the U.S. National Institute on Alcohol Abuse and Alcoholism at www.niaaa.nih.gov or a similar government-sponsored Web site.

The information contained in this section is based on the information published in one of my own local sources of information, The Australian Wine Research Institute—Wine and health information. Further information can be found on their Web site: www.awri.com.au.

The additives and preservatives used in winemaking

Winemaking, especially on a commercial scale, incorporates the use of both additives and preservatives. Their use is necessary not only to aid winemaking, but also to protect against exposure to oxygen and bacteria, both of which can severely affect the quality of the grapes and the finished product.

Additives are used in winemaking to assist fermentation, prevent bacteria developing in both the juice and wine, correct acidity, and prevent or remove any unwanted colors, flavors, or smells. Similarly, preservatives protect wine from prolonged exposure to oxygen and bacterial spoilage as a result of naturally forming yeasts in the vineyard, or from winemaking equipment that hasn't been adequately cleaned.

The two most commonly used preservatives in winemaking are sulfur dioxide (220/224) and sorbic acid (200/202). And while there is no such thing as a completely preservative-free wine, organic wines and wines made from organically grown grapes will have reduced amounts of both additives and preservatives.

If you're asthmatic and your condition is sulfur-sensitive, see further down the page.

Wine and allergy sufferers

Allergy sufferers should proceed with caution. Prior to bottling, most wine is fined, or filtered, to remove impurities. With many modern fining agents derived from egg, fish, milk, and nut products, it's really important if you do have allergies that you check the packaging first for warning statements—now a legal requirement in many countries. If you have a known allergy, consume wine at your own risk, since traces of these products may remain in the wine.

Those with yeast allergies should be able to consume wine without reaction, but proceed with caution. While all wine is fermented from grape juice using yeast product, only a trace amount would remain in the finished wine. No studies, however, have shown wine to cause life-threatening allergy symptoms in allergy sufferers.

Wine and asthmatics

Asthma can be triggered in a number of ways. If your asthma is triggered by sulfur compounds, such as sulfur dioxide, you should not consume wine. If your asthma is not triggered by this, wine is unlikely to precipitate an attack. Sulfur-sensitive asthmatics should seek out wines with reduced amounts of sulfur dioxide. For example, organic wines will contain around 50 percent less sulfur than other commercial wines. Avoid bulk wine, such as cask wine and wine flagons—both of which are likely

to include increased amounts of sulfur dioxide.

Wine and heart conditions

If you have a heart condition, you should consume wine in moderation—provided it doesn't react with any prescribed medication that you might be taking. While the consumption of wine isn't recommended, those of you with high blood pressure controlled by medication may consume wine in moderation, provided your blood pressure is stable. Check with a medical professional if you are worried at all.

Wine and celiac disease

Products and additives that contain gluten are not allowed to be used in the production of still wine. While sparkling wine produced in Australia doesn't include any additives containing gluten, Champagne and other sparkling wines may include a spirit produced from wheat grain, making them unsuitable for celiacs.

It is also important for celiacs to avoid any fortified wines and sherries that may contain caramel product, identified as additive 150.

Wine and diabetes

Diabetics can consume wine in moderation if their diabetes is controlled, but it should always be drunk with food. Alcohol can cause your blood sugar to crash (hypoglycemia), especially if you have insulin- or medication-dependent diabetes. Low sugar or dry wines are recommended for diabetics—this includes most still and sparkling wines and dry sherry. Sweet still wines, dessert wines, and fortified wines should be avoided. As always, talk to your doctor for further advice about your own circumstances.

Wine and pregnancy

This is one of the most controversial topics in wine and health, and there is certainly no shortage of conflicting opinions. The National Health and Medical Research Council's *Australian Alcohol Guidelines* (October 2001) recommends that women who are planning to get pregnant, or are pregnant, drink no more than one standard drink per day. In 2005 the U.S. Surgeon General stated that a pregnant woman should not drink alcohol, while the U.K. Department of Health, since 2007, has recommended that pregnant women should ideally abstain and should never exceed 1–2 units a maximum of once or twice a week. Consult your local source of governmental advice and your own doctor for further advice.

Certainly, pregnant women should never become intoxicated, as alcohol in the bloodstream will also enter that of an unborn child, possibly affecting its birth weight and increasing the risk of FAS or fetal alcohol syndrome. FAS is characterized by three diagnostic criteria: reduced growth, craniofacial and neurological abnormalities, and certain cardiac, central nervous system, limb, and urogenital abnormalities. FAS occurs in babies born to mothers who regularly drank heavy amounts of alcohol during their pregnancy— that is, six or more standard drinks per day and possibly including other drugs such as caffeine and nicotine.

If you are pregnant, or thinking about starting a family, please do some research for yourself and consult your medical practitioner.

Alcohol and the individual

Alcohol affects us all in different ways, and size, weight, genetic makeup, and ethnicity will affect our tolerance levels. Once alcohol enters your bloodstream, there are two steps in your body's process for breaking it down.

Step one involves converting alcohol to acetaldehyde, while step two converts acetaldehyde into acetate. At this point, it can then be removed from the body by the kidneys.

Some Asian groups contain a proportion of individuals with an inactive gene preventing step two —the conversion of acetaldehyde to acetate. Because of this, the level of acetaldehyde can be as much as ten times higher than normal in some people before the body finally begins to break it down. The effects of having this inactive gene include an increased heartbeat, facial flushing, headaches, nausea, vomiting, drowsiness, and low blood pressure. These symptoms can often occur after just one standard drink. Your doctor can give you advice if you are concerned that this may apply to you.

Wine and teeth

Consuming a moderate amount of wine should not damage your teeth —although, largely because of my job, I've spent more money at the dentist than I care to remember.

Most wines have a pH value of somewhere between 3.0 and 3.8, making them quite acidic. Similarly, red wine contains anthocyanin and tannin compounds that, depending on how much you consume, can stain your teeth.

Because of these two factors, winemakers and professionals who taste on a regular basis run the risk of chemical erosion, staining, increased sensitivity, and the risk of decay to both teeth and restorative materials. Basically, if you're planning on a career in wine, make sure that you have a good dentist and dental cover on your health insurance!

Wine and vegans and vegetarians

How you define your vegetarianism will determine whether or not you can drink wine. Wine can be clarified using egg albumin (egg protein), casein (milk protein), gelatin (beef tissue), or isinglass (fish tissue), all of which are compounds derived from animals. That said, all clarifying agents are removed from the wine prior to bottling and will not be traceable in the finished product. Make sure that you refer to the packaging for any warnings.

Headaches and hangovers

Many of us will have experienced a hangover. Alcohol acts on various parts of the body in various ways.

The most common side effect of alcohol consumption is a headache characterized by a throbbing pain at the front of your head. I'm sure there are those of you who know what I'm talking about!

This happens as a result of your blood-alcohol concentration. More alcohol in your bloodstream means a greater buildup of acetaldehyde once alcohol has been broken down by your liver. In short, acetaldehyde is a highly concentrated toxic compound that transfers very quickly from the bloodstream to fluids in the brain and the spinal cord. It irritates the membrane surrounding the brain and the spinal cord, resulting in a throbbing pain at the front of your head.

We all have our different hangover remedies—mine is to try to drink at least one quart of water before I go to bed, which seems to work— most of the time . . .

What is moderation?

Many experts say that the regular and moderate consumption of wine is good for you, provided you are healthy to begin with. But what is moderation? Medical and scientific studies generally define drinking in moderation as drinking approximately two standard drinks per day.

A standard drink is defined as 100ml (3.4 oz.)of wine. Both consumption and frequency are important. This is averaged out, meaning that, just because you haven't had a drink for six days doesn't mean you can have 14 drinks in one go. Doing so is defined as binge drinking and can significantly increase your blood pressure, along with your chances of having a heart attack or stroke.

With moderate drinking (two standard drinks per day), the risk of developing cardiovascular disease and your risk of death from cardiovascular disease is greatly reduced.

What are polyphenolic compounds?

Polyphenols are derived from the winemaking process. They are antioxidants that come from the skins and pips of grapes and contribute to a wine's color, aroma, and structure.

As the juice from red grapes remains in contact with both its skins and its pips during production, red wine ends up on average being six times higher in its polyphenol content than white wine. While a lot of research is still being done on the health benefits of polyphenols, it is thought that they may contribute to a decreased risk of cardiovascular or heart disease.

What is resveratrol?

Resveratrol is a natural antibiotic, a chemical compound produced by the vine in response to fungal infection. While a lot of research is still being done, it is also thought that resveratrol has a number of health benefits that include possibly delaying the onset of Parkinson's, Alzheimer's, and other forms of dementia, as well as inhibiting the development of

cardio fibrosis—a condition that reduces the heart's pumping efficiency. Perhaps most significantly, resveratrol may prevent and repair damage to DNA associated with the initiation of cancer, as well as acting to prevent the growth and spread of cancerous cells. Time will tell.

The French Paradox

In 1991, CBS's *60 Minutes* reported the phenomenon that has come to be known as the French Paradox. Its findings caused people to once again look more closely at wine's positive and medicinal qualities.

It focuses on the fact that the diet of the southern French—which includes a high proportion of cheese, butter, eggs, organ meats, and other cholesterol-laden foods, and is similar to that of the U.S.— would seem to be linked to increased levels of heart disease was, in fact, leading to longer life expectancies.

With considerably fewer deaths related to heart disease, the difference was linked by some to the fact that, while Americans drink 2.03 gallons of wine per person per year, the residents of southern France drink a whopping 16 gallons of wine per person per year. –

Wine and driving

Permitted blood alcohol levels vary from country to country. If you own or regularly drive a car, it is your responsibility to know what that permitted level is, as well as to know your limitations. I strongly recommend that, if you intend to drink at all, you do not drive.

glossary

Acidity This is needed in wine as a natural preservative as well as to balance *flavor*, adding a crisp, mouth-watering character.

Alcohol This is also needed in wine as a natural preservative as well as to balance *flavor*, adding a full and warming character.

Aroma(tics) The smells found in a wine, which are defined by the grape variety from which the wine is made.

Appellation Defines the controlled geographical origin of a wine.

Balance How *acid*, *alcohol*, fruit, and *tannin* in a wine work together. The aim is to produce the most satisfactory *mouthfeel*.

Barrel-fermentation When the fermentation of alcohol takes place in wood rather than in a tank or a vat.

Bitter(ness) An unpleasant taste in wine detected on the *finish*, especially noticeable in *oxidized* wines.

Clean What a wine should be, with no hint of a fault and/or bad *aroma* or taste.

Complex(ity) Found in top-class wines, when there is a multitude of *aromas* and *flavors*.

Corked/Cork taint A wine fault that, in degrees, strips a wine of all its flavor, and can give musty *aromas*.

Cuvée Now commonly used French term for a blend of *vintages*, used especially for sparkling wines.

Developed How mature the wine is and whether it is ready to drink.

Dry A wine that has been fermented completely, so that there is no *residual sugar* left.

Fermentation The work of *yeast* on the grape juice, turning *sugar* into *alcohol*.

Filtering Occurs after *fining* to completely clarify a wine of *yeast* or *lees*, etc., but can strip *complexity* from a wine.

Fining Initial clarification of wine using a protein, or a similar substance, which precipitates out unwanted solids.

Finish What you can taste and sense after swallowing a wine (see also *length*).

Full-bodied A wine that fills the *palate*. This feeling relates to the amount of *alcohol* and fruit in a wine.

Generic A wine that is not from a specific grape variety or *appellation*.

Grip A wine that has firm *structure* from *tannin*. More commonly found in red wine.

Hollow A wine that lacks *balance* of fruit, when length of flavour is short.

Lees *Sediment* at the bottom of a barrel, tank, or vat consisting of *yeast* and other solids.

Length The length of time you can taste and sense the wine after swallowing; the longer, the better the wine.

Magnum A large 1.5 liter bottle containing two 75cl bottles of wine.

Malolactic fermentation After the first *fermentation*, usually in red wine, which turns harsh malic acid into softer lactic acid.

Mouthfeel Related to *balance* and how a wine feels on the *palate*.

Noble rot A rot that shrivels and concentrates sugar in grapes, producing lusciously sweet wines.

Nonvintage A wine that is a blend of different vintages, most commonly sparkling wines.

Nose Wine-tasting jargon for the smell of a wine.

Oaked A wine that has been matured in oak barrels, or a cheaper method, such as contact with oak chips.

Oxidized A fault in wine when it has been overexposed to oxygen. Will display an unpleasant stale smell and taste.

Palate Wine-tasting jargon for the mouth.

Polyphenols The pigments found in red grape skins: *tannins* and anthocyanins.

Residual sugar Any *sugar* left in a wine that has not been *fermented*.

Ripe(ness) A wine that tastes rich and naturally sweet, thanks to fully ripe grapes.

Round Related to *balance*; when a wine is smooth with no hard edges.

Sediment Found in a mature wine, especially one that has not been *filtered*.

Sommelier A wine waiter or waitress in a restaurant.

Structure Related to how a wine is "built" and if it can age.

Sugar Contained naturally in grapes and *fermented* into alcohol. Any left in wine is called *residual sugar*.

Tannin A *polyphenol* that breaks down in wine as it ages, found mainly in red wine. Adds a drying, *grippy* character.

Terroir A French term used to describe a character found in wine given by the place where it is made.

Ullage The space between the top of the wine and its container, usually a bottle, which increases as wine ages.

Varietal Relates to a wine made from a specific grape variety.

Viticulture The practice of growing grapes and vineyard management.

Vinification The practice of winemaking.

Vintage The year the grapes used in a wine were grown and harvested.

Volatile (acidity) Usually a fault in wine when the *acidity* is unbalanced and harsh.

Weight Related to *body*, both red and white wine can range from light to heavy in weight.

Yeast Used in the *fermentation* of wine, and can be natural (on the grape skin) or cultured.

Yield The amount of wine made relating to the weight of grapes harvested from a given area of vineyard.

index

Figures in *italic* indicate captions.

acetaldehyde 171
acetic acid 86
acidity 85, 89, 96, 102, 105, 114,
    112, 125, 126, *126*, 169, 174
    and aging 143, 148
additives 36, 53, 169
aging 139
    how wine changes over time
        143, *143*
    long-term 148, *148*
    tracking a wine's
        development 146
    two-year-old wines 146, *146*
    wine's molecular structure
        139, 140
    young wines 143, 144, *144*
air 132, 135, 139
alcohol 174
    alcohol dependence,
        alcoholism 168, 169
    alcoholic strength 33, 36, 85
    and body 89
    excessive 53
    winetasting 85
allergy 170
Alsace vintages 49
altitude 34
Alzheimer's disease 173
Amarone 104, 111
anthocyanin 140, 173
Argentina 34, 50, 55
Asian food 114, 125
asthmatics 170
auctions *25*, 153, *153*
    bargains 25
    benefits 25
    inspecting the wines 25
    tips 27
Australia 34, 50
Australian Wine Research
    Institute 169

bad wine 140, 161
balance 83, 89, 94, 96, 102,
    148, 174
Banyuls 104
Barbera 144
bargains
    auction 25
    Internet 24
    supermarket 18
barrels, oak 85
Beaujolais (Gamay) 144
beef 111-112
biodynamics 53, 54, *54*, 55
body 85, 89
Bordeaux *78*
    bottle shape 37
    vintages 49
bottles
    PET plastic 55
    shape 37, *37*
    size 37, *37*
bouquet 89
brettanomyces 53, 86
brokers 162, *162*
budget
    auctions 27

restaurant 28, *28*
bulk buying 162
Burgundy *78*
    bottle shape 37
    vintages 49
buying wine *see* investment

Cabernet 148
Cabernet Sauvignon 111, 118, 129
caramelization 140
carbon-neutral wines 55
cardio fibrosis 173
Carignan 112
casein (milk protein) 172
cava 144
Cecchini, Dario 112
Celiac disease 170
cellar 132, 151
    cellaring options 157
    location 154, *154*, 156
Chablis 148
chain wine stores 20, *20*
Champagne
    bottle shape 37
    flutes 65
    and foods 122, 125
    Heidsieck "Goût Americain" 153
    nonvintage 148
    opening 70, *70*
    serving temperature 69
    vintage 49, 148
Chardonnay 105, 109, 111, 114,
    125-126, 146, 148
cheese 112, *112*
chicken 101, 125-126
Chile 34, 50, 55
chili wines 114
clarifying agents 172
clean wine 89, 174
climate 34, 49
closed wine 89
cork taint 38, 41, 43, 86, 174
corks 38, *38*, 41, 43, 139
    agglomerate 41, *41*
    alternative closures 38, 41, *41*
    brittle 156
    broken 74
    faulty wines 38
    keeping moist 156
    liking/disliking 38
    synthetic 41, *41*
corkscrews 58, 63, *63*, 72, *72*
counterfeit wine 160, *162*
crown seals 41

decanters/decanting 58, 67,
    74, 137
    allowing the wine to
        "breathe" 67
    choosing a decanter 67
    how to decant 67
    sediment 67
diabetics 170-171
Dolcetto 144
drill-down cellar *154*, 157
drinking and driving 173
drinking wine 58-59
dry wines 104, 112, 174
duck 126, 129

duty 47
egg albumin (egg protein) 172
Eiswein 104
ethyl acetate 86
Europe 34, 50
European food 114, 125

Fairtrade wine 55, *55*
FAS (foetal alcohol syndrome) 171
fermentation, barrel 140, 174
fertilizers 53
filtering 53, 174
fining agents 36, 174
fish 109, 122, *122*
flavor 83, 94, 101, *101*, 105, 111, 112
    and aging 143
food and wine matching 28,
    94, 106
    acidity 96, 102
    the best food and wine
        partners 122-129
    by country 114, *114*
    by ingredient 109, *109*, 111,
        112, *112*
    by season 117, *117*, 118, *118*
    flavor 96, 101, *101*
    the rules 96
    sweetness 96, 104, *104*
    tannin 96, 103, *103*
    temperature 96, 105, *105*
    weight 96, 98, *98*
fortified wines 69, 144
French Paradox 168, 173
fruit aromas 77, 80, 89, 143
fruity taste 89
fungicides 53

game 109
gelatin (beef tissue) 172
gelato 129
German wines
    acidity/sweetness
        levels 85
    bottle shape 37
    Riesling 125
    vintages 49
    Gewürztraminer 114, 144
glassware 58, 61, 65, *65*
    cleaning 65
gluten 170
glycerol 89
goat cheese 125
gold medals 36
good/bad years 48-49
Grenache 111, 112, 146
Gurney, Dan 70

half bottles 28
hangovers 172
headaches 172
heart conditions 170, 173
herbicides 53
    bargains and range 20
    service 20
humidity 132, 154, 156, 157
hydrogen sulfide 86
ice bucket 105
ice cream 129

independent wine
    merchants 22, *22*
insurance 162
International Wine
    Challenge 36
Internet
    absentee auction bids 27
    bargains and range 24
    buying wine 24
    reviews 18
    service 24
    tips 14
investment 25, 159
    the "don'ts" of buying wine
        165, *165*
    the "dos" of buying wine
        162, *162*
    factors influencing wine
        value 161
    for financial gain 160
    for love 160
    risks 160
isinglass (fish tissue) 172
Italian vintages 49

lamb 111, 129
laying down bottles 156
leftover wine 136-137
length 83, 89, 174
light sensitivity 132, 154, 156
Liqueur Muscat 129

Madeira 104
magazines: wine columns 18
mailing lists 22
Malbec 112
marsala 194
Marsanne 146
Maury 104
Merlot 111, 114, 144
moderate consumption 172
Moscato 104, 129
Mourvèdre 112
mouthfeel 89, 143, 174
mozzarella 126
Muscatel *78*, 104
mutton 111
myths 33

National Health and Medical
    Research Council 171
Nebbiolo 109, 146
Negroamaro 111
Nero d'Avola 111
New World 34, 50, 144, 146
New Zealand 34, 50
newspapers: wine columns 18
nitrogen 136, 137
noble rot 174

oak chips 53, 174
Old World 34, 43, 50, 144
olfactory nerve 80
opening
    a bottle of bubbly 70, *70*
    a bottle of wine 72, *72*, 74
organic certification 53

organic wine 53, *53*
oxidation 38, 41, 43, 78, 86, 135, 137, 140, 156, 174
oxygen 43, 86, 135, 137, 139, 140, 143, 169
oxygen/wine ratio 37, 137
oysters 122

packaging 47, 55, 170, 172
Parkinson's disease 173
Pedro Ximénez (PX) 104, 129
Penfolds Grange 151
pesticides 53
pH value 172
pink wines 109, 144
    see also rosé wines
Pinot Grigio 144
Pinot Noir 109, 114, 126, 129, 146
pizza 126
plastic taint 41
plum pudding 129
polyphenols 140, 143, 172, 174
pork 111
port 49, 104
Portuguese vintages 49
poultry 109
pregnancy 171
preservatives 169
price of wine *46*, 47
Primitivo 111
production
    careless 140
    costs 47
    and wine value 161
prosecco 144
provenance 162

race, and the effect of alcohol 171
rarity 47
recycling 55
red wines
    acidity *126*
    color and aging 143
    and foods 109, 111
    looking at 78, *78*
    oxidation 86
    polyphenols 140, 143
    seasons 117, 118
    serving temperature 69
    sleepers 148
    tannin 103, *126*, 143, 173
    and temperature change 156
    two-year-old 146
    young 144
refrigeration 136, 137, 157

region 34, 161
reputation of wine producer 33, 34, 47, 161
restaurants: winebuying 28-29
    consult the sommelier 28
    half bottles and glasses 28
    identify styles you like 28
    matching wine and food 28
    tips 28
    your budget 28, *28*
resveratrol 173
reverse osmosis 53
Rhône vintages 49
Riesling *78*, 104, 114, 125, 148
Rioja *78*
rosé wines
    looking at 78
    and mozzarella 126
    seasons 117, 118
    serving temperature 69
    young 144
    see also pink wines

Sangiovese 103, 111, 126, 146
Sassicaia 112
Sauternes 104
Sauvignon Blanc 112, 118, 125, 144
screw caps 38, 41, *41*, 43, *43*
seasons 105, 117, *117*, 118, *118*
secondary aromas 143
sediment 67, 74, 140, 143, 174
Semillon 148
Semillon/Sauvignon blends 144
service
    chain wine stores 20, *20*
    independent wine merchants 22
    supermarkets 18
serving wine 61
shellfish 109
sherry 49, 69, *78*, 104, 109, 122, 144, 170, 171
Shiraz *78*, 111, 112, 146
shopping around 162
smoke taint 53
soil 34
sommelier 28, 174
sorbic acid 169
South Africa 34, 50, 55
Spanish vintages 49
sparkling wines 70, *70*, 144, 170, 171
Steiner, Rudolph 54
Stelvin closure 41
stoppers
    glass 41, *41*
    spring-loaded 136
    storage, wine 61

see also cellar
sugar 104, 140, 174
sulfides 170
sulfur dioxide 36, 53, 169, 170
supermarkets 18, *18*
    bargains 18
    service 18
    shopability 18
sweet wines 85, 104, 112, 170
    sleepers 148
sweetness 85, 89, 96, 104, *104*, 105, 114, 125
Syrah 146

tannic wines 89, 114
tannin 96, 111, 140, 143, 174
    definition 85
    helps balance wine 89
    levels in wine 103, 105, 126, *126*, 148, 173
    and sediment 140, 143
tastebuds 85, *85*
    acidity 85
    alcohol 85
    body 85
    sweetness 85
    tannin 85
    texture 85
tastings
    chain wine stores 20
    language 89
    pre-auction 27
    using eyes 77, 78, *78*
    using mouth 77, 83
    using nose 77, 80
    vineyard 30
    visual aid *89*
TCA (2,4,6-Trichloranisole) 36, 41
technology versus tradition 50
teeth 171-172
temperature 96, 105, *117*
    cellar 154, 156, 157
    chilling wines 69
    seasons 105
    serving 61, 69
    what it does to wine 105
Tempranillo 111, 146
terroir 50, 174
texture 83, 85, 94, 96, 102, 103, 114, 112
    and aging 143
Thai food 125
Tokay 104
tools 102
Touriga Nacional 111
Trockenbeerenauslese 104

Uruguay 34, 50

U.S. National Institute on Alcohol Abuse and Alcoholism (NIAAA) 169
U.S. 34, 50
vacuum pumps 137
Valpolicella Classico 111
varieties 34, 47
VAT (tax) 47
veal 111
vegans 172
vegetarianism 172
Verdejo 144
Verdelho 144
vibration 132, 154, 156
vinegar 132, 135
vineyards 30, *30*, 34
vino-seal 41, *41*
vintage 36, 47, 49, *49*, 174
    and wine value 161
Viognier 114, 109, 146
viscosity 89
volatile acidity 53, 174

weather 49, *49*
weight 96, 98, *98*, 104, 105, *117*, 112, 174
well-being 168-173
white wines
    caramelization 140
    and foods 109, 111
    looking at 78, *78*
    oxidation 86
    seasons 117, 118
    serving temperature 69
    sleepers 148
    and temperature change 156
    two-year-old 146
    young 144
wine by the glass 28
wine critics 162
wine faults 80, 86, *86*
    see also cork taint; oxidation
wine guides 18
wine labels
    additives 34, 36
    alcohol 34, 36
    design 33, 36, *36*
    gold medals 36
    producer 33, 34, *34*
    region and vineyard 34, *34*
    variety 34, *34*
    vintage *34*, 36
wine merchants 160, 162, *162*
wine prices 160, 161
wine waiters or waitresses 28

young wines 143, 144, *144*

Zinfandel 112

cheers

There's no way this book would ever have been possible without the enormous contributions, generosity, love, blood, sweat —and, in some cases, tears—tipped in by the following people.

Kicking off with Chris Terry, Matt Utber and their respective teams, Jade, Lisa, and all the crew at The Plant, and Danny Tracy at Chris Terry Photography.

To my extended family at Mitchell-Beazley, in London, U.K.; Alison Gough, David Lamb, Becca Spry, Hilary Lumsden, Georgina Atsiaris, Yasia Williams-Leedham, Tim Foster, and in the same breath to Louise Sherwin-Stark and Kate Taperell at Hachette Australia.

To those that gave more than just time, including the lovely Planeta family—Palermo, Sicily, Phil Sexton, and Giant Steps—Healsville, Victoria, Christies London, Majestic, David Gleave MW, Philip Rich, and The Prince Hotel, Melbourne, Australia.

To my team; Debbie Catchpole and Verity O'Brian at Fresh Partners and Lisa Sullivan at One Management.

To my extended family: Fifteen Group (London, Cornwall, Amsterdam, and Melbourne), Jonathan Downey and Match Group (London, Ibiza, New York, Charmonix, and Melbourne), Frank van Haandel and Roger Fowler, and Trevor Eastment at XYZ Networks.

And last but not least, to those behind the scenes; Mum, Drew, Caroline, Jessie, Eve, Anne, Thommo, Gin, Camilla & Felix, Tobe, George, Randy, Pip, Gyros, BP, CC & GG, Jamie & Jools, Danny McCubbin, Stuart Gregor, Cam Mackenzie, Andy Frost, The Jones, Cooper-Terry, and Utber clans.

From the bottom of my heart, thank you. Mx